Landscape Gardening
and the Choice of Plants

Landscape Gardening and the Choice of Plants

FRÉDÉRIQUE and MARC TANGUY

translated by Alan Sheridan

University Press of Virginia, Charlottesville

Originally published as *La composition des espaces verts et le choix des végétaux*
© 1981 Editions J.-B. Ballière

THE UNIVERSITY PRESS OF VIRGINIA
Copyright © 1985 by the Rector and Visitors
of the University of Virginia

First published 1985

Library of Congress Cataloging in Publication Data

Tanguy, Frédérique.
  Landscape gardening and the choice of plants.

  Translation of: La composition des espaces verts et
le choix des végétaux.
  Includes index.
    1. Landscape gardening.   2. Landscape architecture.
3. Plants, Ornamental.   I. Tanguy, Marc.   II. Title.
SB472.T2713   1985   635.9   85-3344
ISBN 0-8139-1058-7

Printed in the United States of America

Contents

Introduction

In acquiring the skills required in the practice of his craft, the budding landscape gardener is confronted by problems that require not only knowledge but also the ability to think through the problems and to apply whatever experience he or she has gained.

The design of a park or garden and the choice of plants are two such areas of difficulty.

There are few books on these subjects, while there are a great many very good ones on the history of gardens, on the rules of design, on the techniques for carrying out one's designs, on the characteristics of plants, etc.

We have tried to bring our experience as teachers and practitioners to bear on these two points. We have tried not to provide "recipes," but rather to outline a rational method of approaching problems.

If this book encourages readers to look at gardens and plants with a new eye, it will have served its purpose.

Landscape Gardening
and the Choice of Plants

I. Design

In approaching any design project, one must first study the facts, the données of the problem; one must then formulate one's findings; only then is one really in a position to make choices, to propose solutions, in other words, to work out a plan.

All this is obvious enough, and no one would deny it. Yet, when it comes to parks and gardens, the same procedure is often ignored. "Gardening is different," people say.

The "program" is almost always the first thing to be attacked, either because it is inadequate or, on the contrary, because it exists at all.

The facts to be taken into consideration are too numerous, elusive, or ill-defined. How many landscape gardeners have said, or heard someone else say, things like: "We gardeners work with materials that are difficult to handle, because they are living things"; "the client never knows what he wants"; "one doesn't even know where the drains are"; "the survey plan of the site is only approximate," etc. There is often something to such remarks, but they sometimes serve to justify gaps and inadequacies at the planning stage.

If the problem is not thought through, there is no real choice, for all too often "improvisation" amounts to doing the same thing over and over again.

The second danger, in our opinion, is to regard the program, when it has the merit of existing at all, as simply a constraint on creation. This attitude leads more or less to ignoring it, or at least to ignoring whatever one happens to regard as "impossible" about it.

The inexperienced landscape gardener then finds himself at his desk faced with an unpleasant alternative: either he must think up something new, or he must submit to the constraints of the program.

This is a negative attitude, and in order not to fall into it, we would suggest another, more optimistic one that might be summed up as follows:

> rather than subjecting oneself to the program, try to exploit its possibilities
>
> rather than feeling inhibited by the constraints, try to use them as the basis for ideas
>
> finally, even if the givens are incomplete, go back to the basic approach—analysis, formulation of givens, proposals, etc.

A. Analysis of the Components of the Program

The first stage in our work, then, is to analyze all the available information about the project.

This information is of various kinds and may concern such different matters as topography and finance. The amount of information depends on the nature and scope of the project, but also on how complete and detailed the information provided may be.

The client is the one responsible for drawing up this program. But very often, especially in the case of smaller projects, the prime contractor and even the builder have to make up for its inadequacies by assisting in its formulation. That at least is what happens in practice.

In the early stages, the analysis of the program must be carried out as objectively as possible, in order to avoid the premature choice of a particular design concept, before one has become thoroughly familiar with all the givens. Is not the garden always a compromise between the terrain, with all its possibilities and limitations, and the client, with his needs and requirements?

1. The Terrain

We prefer the term *terrain* to *site*, for it embraces not only the latter term but also its environment, and it is precisely the whole that must be taken into account.

This analysis of the terrain must be made in two ways:

1. by studying the documents
2. by visiting the site

a. The documents

There is really no limit to the number of documents involved: everything depends on the size of the project.

They should normally be provided by the client. The main documents to be considered are plans, studies, and public planning documents.

(1) Plans

Local plans make it possible to place the site not only in its immediate environment but possibly within a broader context (neighborhood, town), depending on the size of the area affected by the project. They also tell one about the existing facilities (roads, drains, and electricity cables; sports and educational facilities; public services; shops; etc.).

The plan of the present state of the site is to be found in most files. This is the basic document. Existing vegetation may be marked on it. Everything appearing on such a plan may or may not be to scale.

The plans of existing or planned buildings and service networks will complement our knowledge of the existing state of the site.

(2) Studies

These may concern:

—The nature of the soil, knowledge of which ought to be indispensable in planning a garden and the choice of plants
—The nature of the subsoil, which will determine the foundations required, what is feasible in terms of earthworks, and drainage of rainwater
—The climatic, and above all microclimatic, givens, which may have an influence on the choice of new plants
—A visual study of the terrain, which is always very important and often neglected. This is almost always carried out by the designer himself and is seldom included in the documents provided by the client
—A study of the fauna, which is justified in the case of minor elements of natural terrains, for instance

(3) Public planning documents

These provide information on the administrative and legal situation of the site. These regulations and obligations are contained in the deeds of sale, the articles and conditions of sale, the land-use map, etc. They may influence the siting, the nature, and the appearance of facilities, the planting, etc.

b. Site Visits

However complete the file may be, it is no substitute for a visit or several visits to the site.

Such visits make it possible to check the accuracy of the documents, to complement them, and to appreciate the possibilities of the terrain.

—Checking the accuracy of the documents: very often changes, sometimes very important ones, take place in the course of the works (the erection of a building, changes in dimensions, etc.). Revised documents or plans are not always sent to those concerned.

—Complementing the documents: the file is, as we have said, sometimes very small, and it is therefore up to the designer to fill it out, which will lead him in some cases to make studies of topography, the vegetation, the soil (by observing the spontaneous vegetation or, for greater precision, by taking samples), etc.

—Appreciating the possibilities of the terrain.

What this amounts to in fact is a visual analysis of the terrain; an appreciation that will therefore necessarily be rather subjective.

It will consist of noting down interesting or unpleasant views, axes that should be preserved or eliminated, areas that form a homogeneous visual unity, precise points that attract attention by their positive or negative qualities.

There are terrains that have a particular atmosphere, the result of a multitude of details that must be absorbed, while not losing sight of the fact that this terrain will be altered and that many of these details will disappear in the course of the work. Views are an example of this, so one can see the importance in this case of acquainting oneself first with the documents relevant to the project.

This study of the possibilities of the terrain may take the form of photographs, montages of photographs, sketches, etc.

2. Needs

a. Definition of the needs and role of the client

Certain needs and requirements are laid down by the client: they constitute what is often called the program.

Since the project must respond to the needs that have been expressed, a good definition of those needs is therefore indispensable to a good design.

But defining needs is not such a simple matter. In the case of a public park, for instance, it involves defining the future needs of populations whose characteristics are not always known with sufficient precision or accuracy. Moreover, these populations change. This presupposes, in many cases, making a study based upon hypothetical, rather than real, needs.

When the client is assisted by specialized technical services, the brief is often the work of these services, which may themselves require, in the case of large-scale works or those of an unusual type, the assistance of other specialists (sociologists, advisory landscape designers, psychologists, etc.), or firms or departmental units specializing in such matters.

In the case of public or collective projects, attempts are sometimes made to involve the future users in formulation of the program. Such attempts are not always successful, for it is a matter of defining not only personal needs but also collective needs, and in this field, the future user has little experience in the matter. But in spite of disappointments, one must persevere in an approach that involves consultation.

The designer is often involved in drawing up the program in the case of public parks. In the case of private gardens, however, the designer almost always belongs to the team or firm involved and is therefore able to conceive of the program as a whole. This apparent freedom must not be regarded as an advantage, for it is a cause not only of much wasted time and uncertainty but also of conflicts and gaps between the supposed needs and requirements of the client and his real ones.

b. Nature and quantification of needs

The first step to be taken by the client is to define the kind of park or garden that he wants to create. This is often fairly obvious when the space in question is subsidiary to the needs of some building or group of buildings (gardens forming part of a school, of a residential or office complex). But sometimes the client has to make a choice between several possibilities, and the wishes expressed by the users—the possibilities of the site perhaps, or a rational study of the needs of the future population—will then determine the solution.

Each type of park or garden must respond to more or less precise needs. Again, it is a study of the population affected that will make it possible to specify the needs qualitatively and quantitatively. It is essential to know the number, age, and sociooccupational background of this population. Such information will form the basis of a specification, first, of the needs and, second, of the nature and quantity of the elements necessary to satisfy those needs. To assist in doing this, the client has at his disposal norms, studies, regulations, or, on occasion, his previous experience.

One must not forget the changing character of needs. A population changes, and if it stays in the same place, sooner or later, the elements will no longer be suitable. One must, therefore, either provide elements that are easy to change (technically and financially) or provide elements that are sufficiently all-purpose that they will be less than entirely satisfactory in all respects, but will last for a long time.

What this amounts to, then, is that we must define the needs and the changes that they may undergo before drawing up a list of the elements to be created.

But we must also broaden the sense of the term *needs*: very often this word refers only to certain material installations corresponding to various activities, for example: playing, sports, picnicking, camping, large gatherings, sitting, resting, walking, etc.

But there are also quite different needs, more elusive or hidden but just as important, the absence of which sometimes explains the relatively light use made of certain parks and gardens that are nevertheless well-equipped. These are, for example:

—needs that might be called "feelings" or "senses"
—a sense of safety (in a garden for children, for relaxation, for picnic areas beside motorways)
—a sense of familiarity (in a garden belonging to a residential complex, etc.)
—a sense of the unknown, of discovery, of the unexpected (in a children's adventure playground, a garden used for exhibitions, or for walking), etc. needs that relate to what might be called "atmosphere"
—a warm, welcoming atmosphere (for a garden at the entrance to an apartment building, an office building, a day nursery, a school)
—an imposing atmosphere (for certain official buildings)
—an atmosphere reminiscent of a particular period (certain private gardens, reconstructions, etc.)
—a dynamic atmosphere (a thoroughfare, for example)

The first type of needs (those associated with activities) readily suggest the type of facilities and elements required.

The next two types of needs (needs associated with "feelings" or "senses" and needs associated with "atmosphere") are much more difficult to satisfy and, in our opinion, differentiate the project coordinator from the landscape gardener, the architect, the town planner, and the decorator. There is a range of ideas that might prove useful, for example: changes in scale, choice of plants, colors and the combination of colors, forms and the combination of forms, effects of light and shade, changes made to the level of the land (and not only for utilitarian purposes), rhythms and oppositions, focal points, brilliances, textures, etc.

c. Formulation of the analysis of needs: The organigram

The designer must make a critical study of the program, as he has already done of the terrain. This study will lead him to specify, to complement, to bring out the gaps or inconsistencies between the needs and the requirements expressed by the client. This stage of his work is usually done directly on the site plan, which enables him at the same time to integrate the givens of the terrain and to arrive very quickly at a schema of functions. His experience enables him to skip one of the stages in the process, which is the formulation of the analysis of needs—in other words, the organigram. The designer who does not have this experience and who follows the same approach sees only the site and its limitations, and forgets the ultimate purpose of the exercise.

How can one visualize this formulation in the clearest possible way? We can make use of organigrams (as used in management studies), which, in drawing up a list of the elements of the program, make it possible to bring out the functional relations existing between those elements. This makes it possible to represent the functions fulfilled by the elements used, and therefore to recognize possible inadequacies, to question some of them as being too expensive, useless, or as serving more than one purpose.

We shall take a very simple, common example: the case of a private garden. This example will enable anyone, however inexperienced, to draw up his own brief.

A youngish professional couple, with two children (six and ten), has had a house built and is seeking advice about the design of the garden, which occupies an area of between 600 and 700 square meters. It is their first garden, and they have only a very vague idea of their needs or of the likely cost of the undertaking. They would like a large terrace, grass, somewhere for the children to play (Ping-Pong, ball). Apart from that, they are quite prepared to leave everything to the designers.

How, with that embryo of a program, can one set about one's task in a rational way?

To begin with, we must imagine the needs of that family, then the functions necessarily bound up with the house, and we shall see whether the facilities anticipated seem adequate or not.

Table 1 shows us that certain elements are very important in terms of the number of functions that they will have to fulfill (e.g., the terrace). Others, not mentioned in the program given by this couple, are indispensable and must be added (reception area, entrance, house). Some others may be interesting suggestions to make

Table 1.   Functions connected with the home

Function	Family needs	Corresponding facilities or elements
	Parents	
Relaxation	relaxing after work, preferably in the sun (evening)	terrace, preferably paved relaxation area, grassed and shaded by vegetation
	resting on days off, preferably in shade (daytime)	
	need for peace and quiet	
Social activities	entertaining friends	paved terrace
	playing with the children	large lawn
	eating—and even cooking—out-of-doors	barbecue corner on paved terrace
Physical activities	gardening (limited)	flower beds, herb garden, bed for cut flowers
	games with the children	large lawn, corner for Ping-Pong
	adults' games	bowls, Ping-Pong
	Children	
relaxation	a quiet area, well out of sight of the grownups	small grassed, shaded area, with wooden shed
Social activities	playing with other children	other games areas (below)
	playing with the parents	large lawn
Physical activities	ball games	lawn Ping-Pong
	individual activities: running, skipping, climbing, hopscotch, etc.	games area, with crossbeam, preferably graveled, fairly out of sight of the grownups
	quiet games (dolls, tea party, shop)	small shaded lawn, with wooden shed
	Uses associated with the life of the house	
Access	pedestrian access from street to garden	gate and garden path, preferably paved
	reception of guests and entrance to house	fairly small, but welcoming area at front of house
Cars	vehicular access from street to garage	gates and drive to garage
	area for turning around or parking cars	graveled area between garage and gates
Utilitarian	log pile	utility area, preferably graveled, out of sight
	drying of clothes	

to the client (children's games in addition to the Ping-Pong installation). On the other hand, we will abandon those that are obviously not realistic (a special area for ball games, for example, because of the area available).

Let us now classify these elements in order of importance, and draw up a theoretical organigram, ignoring the realities of the house and site (fig. 1).

This organigram brings out the role played by the house and reminds us that the private garden is a space that accompanies the house. It also brings out the importance of the relations between the various elements and the need for organization, that is to say, an overall design.

What we have done here, with this example of a private garden, can be done with any type of garden and any area. What is important is the way we approach the problem.

B. Preparation of the Design

Throughout the analysis of the program and in the formulations that we have made of it, we have tried to be as objective as possible. We have made no choice that was not self-evident, in order not to exclude any solution a priori.

We must now bring all the elements of the program together, possibly suggesting others, and must order them according to a clear guiding principle or concept in such a way as to create a unity that is both functional and aesthetic. This is what is called the design concept.

1. Birth of the Design Concept: General Schema of Organization

How does the design concept come about?

Sometimes it emerges, in its main outlines, of its own accord. For example, the site might be particularly interesting in terms of its relief and vegetation, and one is led logically to think in terms of a concept based on landscape. Or again, one's task might be to bring out the importance of a public building by means of an almost "architectural" concept.

But even in cases that appear to be simple, where there is a dominant general idea, one still has a wide range of possibilities at

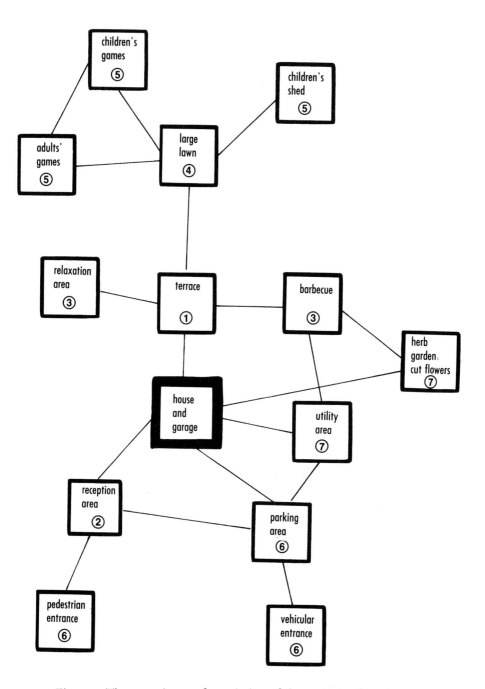

Fig. 1. The organigram: formulation of the analysis of needs.

one's disposal, and one may arrive at relatively different solutions.

Generally speaking, then, one can say that whatever the project, even if one's design concept seems self-evident, one must consider several possibilities before choosing a final solution.

A little imagination is required, of course, but this does not exclude or replace a rational analysis of the problem.

So let us continue with our approach, which tries to be logical, whether or not we have found our design concept.

In drawing up the organigram of needs, we have tried to use stylized symbols (circles and squares, lines and arrows, representing respectively the constituent parts and the relations between them). We are all used to this type of representation when dealing with theoretical problems. So we shall keep these same representations when we are working out our general schema of organization and shall apply them to "points of interest" and to the relations existing between these points. (See fig. 2.)

a. Points of interest
We must now work with two types of elements:

1.   elements corresponding to needs
2.   the noteworthy elements of the terrain (views, plants, presence of water, etc.)

We see that, to begin with, they have different purposes— some are "functional"; others, "decorative." We believe that there is no incompatibility between these two sorts of elements and therefore no point in separating them. All that matters is the interest that they possess and this may be due to either their utility or their decorative quality, or to both. This is why we have called them "points of interest" and have represented them in the same stylized form (circles, squares, etc.) and classified them in order of importance.

But why use circles and squares, when the element in question may be perfectly well represented by its real form and (relative) size? For several reasons:

First, the nature of the element is not always determined at this stage of the design. We may be aware that at a given place we must create a particularly interesting and attractive point of interest

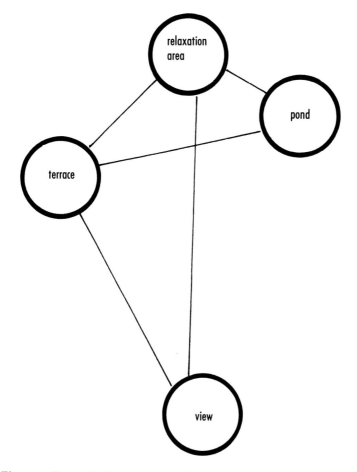

Fig. 2.   General schema of organization.

without having any clear idea yet of what it will be, and that is of no importance whatsoever. This simplification allows us to pursue our work of composition without coming up against this obstacle.

Second, the surface area occupied is a bad representation of the importance of an element. For example, between a grassed multi-purpose play area of 1,000 square meters and a decorative fountain and pool of 20 square meters, the interest, the power of attraction, the visual quality that belong so much more to the second, would be eclipsed to the advantage of the first if one represented the two elements in terms of a scale plan.

Third, on pedagogical grounds, one should avoid—and teach one's students to avoid—taking refuge in figurative representation before deciding on one's design concept, as if the solution of the problem posed will arrive of its own accord.

It is always difficult to reduce an area, a length, a volume, to a point, a circle, a square. But on reflection, this is justified, for does not each element have a strong point, a center of interest, just as every body has a center of gravity? For a stream, a linear element, it might be its source, or the surface of water into which it flows, that will be its principal point of interest.

This simplification ultimately enables us to come up with several schemata very rapidly, to consider a number of solutions before choosing one, and only then to move on to a more figurative stage.

b. Relations

Relations are the links between the points of interest. It is they that create the coherence of the composition, and they are therefore of fundamental importance. Without relations, there is merely a juxtaposition of elements.

The nature of the points of interest implies the nature of the relations. So, just as we had two types of points of interest, we shall have two main types of relations:

1. Functional relations, which can easily be materialized on the site by a circulatory route (path, etc.). We shall therefore call them relations of circulation. One could, of course, carry this analysis farther and subdivide them into relations of pure movement, relations of movement involving activities, etc.
2. Visual relations, which are always important whatever the type of style of space, but above all, of course, when its principal purpose is to be decorative. Here too, visual relations may be divided more specifically into visual relations toward something (a view, a decorative scene, etc.), or against something, in which case it becomes a relation of protection (a visual screen).

Generally speaking, relations have a privileged direction, especially in the case of visual relations, which may have only one, as when the observer sees without being seen. In our diagrams we shall indicate this privileged direction by an arrow. (See fig. 3.) Very often, it is bound up with hierarchization, which we shall deal with in the next chapter.

Often these two types of relation—functional and visual—are superimposed: the first encouraging movement by creating an appeal (visual relation); the second by serving as a support to the first (func-

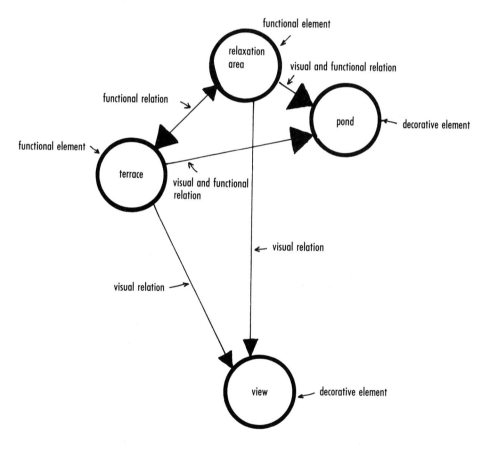

Fig. 3.   Diagram of relations.

tional relation). The two therefore justify, reinforce, one another. They play a dynamic role in the composition.

c. Choice of the dominant element in the composition—hierarchization

If we try to adapt our organigram to the site, a number of elements quickly find their place. They are the ones for which there is little or no choice, for they are self-evident. In placing them, we see that because they are the first to be arranged, they assume an importance that may be disproportionate to their role (e.g., entrances, parking areas, boundary walls, utility areas).

So we very soon become aware of the need to choose our principal point of interest, if we are not to get bogged down in these secondary details. This choice will determine our design concept, and very often our guiding idea, for the nature of the element chosen will govern our principle of organization, and the hierarchization of the other elements.

This being so, it is clear that one may set out with any hypothesis and select at random. In order to guide our choices, one may consider three types of cases:

1. The dominant element in our composition is the principal element in our theoretical organigram, and therefore the most used. If so, we must be quite sure that it is worthy of the importance accorded it or can be made to be so, otherwise it will not fulfill its role. Take, for example, the case of the space belonging to an apartment building. The organigram may show that the parking area is the element used most often, the most important one in the everyday life of the residents. But should we emphasize it by making it the dominant element of our composition?

2. The dominant element in our composition is the most decorative element on the site. In this case, we must be sure that it takes on its full value. If it happens to be an area of water, for example, we must make sure that it is visible, accessible, and possibly that it may be used for some activity. Furthermore, is its position on the site favorable to the principal role that one wants it to play?

3. The dominant element in our composition is some element as yet to be created. It may be purely decorative, and we are brought back to the preceding case, with the added advantage that we can select its situation (at the end of a perspective, at the intersection of two axes, etc.). It might originally have been a secondary element in the organigram that we will later stress by adding to it some important decorative interest.

Very often it is the last case, combining the functional and the visual, that is chosen, and we are then sure of having a dominant element in our composition, one occupying the first place in the hierarchy, that is really attractive.

We have seen that the guiding idea was determined at the moment one chose the dominant element of the composition, and that it often even preceded that choice.

How is that idea to be defined? It comprises:

—the style with which one will deal with the space in question
—the overall configurations of the design that one chooses or that will emerge, taking into account the form and orientation of the site, the buildings, the configurations already existing in the immediate environment
—the principal purpose of the project
—the principle of organization that will emerge in the whole composition

Let us take a few examples:

—In a particular park or garden, one will give more importance to the visual aspects than to the functional, by working with an abundance of plants, arranged in a fluid, nonrigid way, that will form a contrast with the buildings.
—On the other hand, one will give priority to the needs of children by creating a garden at different ground levels, accomodating games, thus isolating the elements and varying the scales.
—Or, again, priority might be given to circulation, thus forming a network of links between the buildings.

To complete our general schema of organization, we must now decide on the hierarchy of the elements, and the relations that will exist between them.

The program is sometimes limited, as are the possibilities of the terrain. The designer must make up for these shortcomings and suggest new points of interest that he will place in such a way as to give balance to the site.

On the other hand, the program is sometimes too extensive, and the site inadequate to accomodate such a large number of installations. In such a case, constituent parts must be made as multipurpose as possible, with functions superimposed upon each other.

Finally, needs are sometimes limited, and the possibilities of the terrain enormous. In such a case, it is likely that the space might be given a wealth of constituent parts of visual interest.

When our schema of general organization is completed, and we are satisfied that it is both coherent and balanced, we can consider the next stage, the sketch.

2. The Emergence of the Design Concept: The Sketch

We now move from our abstract schematic representation to a more realistic one. This intermediary stage will enable us to plot the areas that lie under the influence of the points of interest.

a. Plotting the constituent parts

Some facilities—e.g., those for sports—have fixed dimensions. In the case of children's games and various other games, there are certain advisable norms. For most elements, however, including those that are decorative in nature, we shall have to decide ourselves how much area they require.

This area will be affected by the importance that we wish to give to the element in question, and we have already decided on that. It will be determined in accordance with the scale that we wish to give it; and we must remember that the scale may vary for an individual depending on whether one wishes to apply it to areas of relaxation, of slow movement, of rapid movement, etc. This is not applicable solely to the utility areas, but also, to a lesser degree, to purely decorative points of interest. Depending on whether one will want to give an intimate or an imposing character to a planted area, for example, or whether a particular element will be treated to accompany the movement of motor or pedestrian traffic, it will always be found useful to play with scales.

The area accorded each element will also have to be well proportioned in relation to the overall area of the composition, and especially to the other elements with which it is directly or visually linked.

It is sometimes at this stage that one is led to alter the relations of the schema of organization, for one may now realize the difficulty involved in creating one element on an individual scale when it is connected to another treated on a quite different scale (a public or monumental scale, for example). There is then a problem of proportions to be resolved, and one may be led to abandon the visual relations initially conceived.

When plotting the areas to be occupied by the various constituent parts, one may also, of course, take into account the configuration of the site: the way those areas relate to one another will give coherence to the plan.

Finally, we should remember that the project must be feasible in technical and financial terms, and that even at this stage of the composition, the designer must bear in mind the problem of maintenance.

b. Plotting the areas of influence and the relations

Just as a picture is enhanced by its frame, so a particular element needs a setting, an area that it commands.

In addition to the other elements in its immediate vicinity, this area comprises everything that is in visual relationship to it and enhances it. So visual relations and connections made by movement may also be included within such an area. (See fig. 4.)

In chapter II, devoted to the choice of plants, we call the role that various secondary elements play in enhancing, stressing, or isolating a point of interest the "function of accompaniment."

This area must be decided on for each point of interest. It may be altered later, of course, and need not initially be plotted in too precise a way.

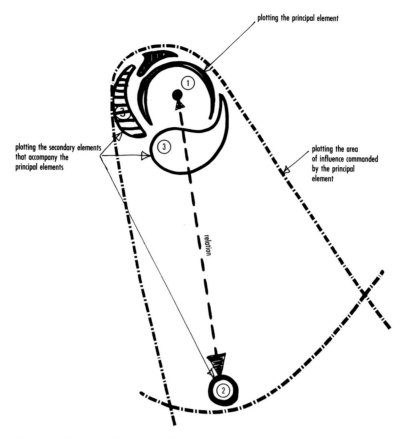

plotting the principal element

plotting the secondary elements that accompany the principal elements

plotting the area of influence commanded by the principal element

relation

Fig. 4. Plotting the area of influence and the relations.

How is it to be done? We must consider the needs that must be fulfilled by the point of interest, its desirable proportions, and with this in view, must work with the help of quick sketches and sections of the space in question. For example, if a path exists solely to facilitate movement from one place to another, it will not, at this stage, be accorded a great deal of surface area, for its outline must appear to be imposed by the constraints of relief, existing plantings, etc. On the other hand, if the design concept has made it an important element, it must be treated as another point of interest and its form, outline, dimensions, and area of influence decided upon.

Visual relations must be represented by straight lines that limit the view to the required angle. It must be remembered that a view need not be panoramic to be interesting, and that it may be more attractive to reveal only parts of it. We should also remember that it may be even more attractive just to hint at it, and to reveal it fully only from another observation point, which might be called the relay observation point, thus encouraging the observer to move on. (See fig. 5.)

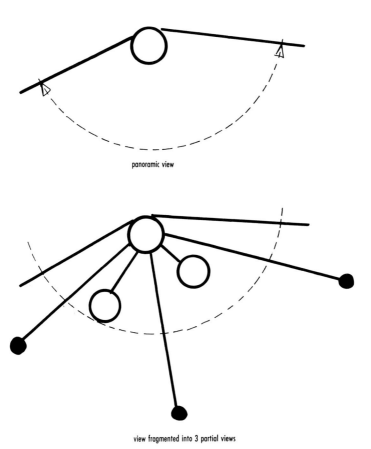

panoramic view

view fragmented into 3 partial views

Fig. 5.   A view need not be panoramic to be interesting, and it may be more attractive to reveal only parts of it.

It is also at this stage that one establishes the successive visual planes that will enhance our view or decorative element.

We have said that we may break up our view, or even replace it by a relay point. It is a good idea to use this technique when too many views are available from the same point. This produces a superimposition of interests, which is a pity, for those interests then run the risk of competing with one another and therefore weakening one another. (See fig. 6.)

c. Intermediary areas

It might be thought that the remaining areas have no purpose. This is not at all so—on the contrary. Their role is very important, although they are often neglected and treated as "filling in."

Such areas will serve as a background, a general framework for the composition as a whole. They will bring out the points of interest and their areas of influence. They will provide, then, a good deal of the unity and general atmosphere by creating a framework against which they will be able to stand out.

Second, these intermediary areas will serve as areas of transition:

—transition between the various elements: one will be able to pass from one element to another, from one function to another, from one scale to another, without being suddenly shocked (when, of course, there is no direct visual relationship between those two elements);

—transition betwen the garden area, in the strict sense, and its environment, which will make it possible, when necessary, to integrate that area into its context.

Third, the intermediary areas provide a certain rest for the eyes: by treating them on a larger scale than the constituent parts themselves, one helps the eye to become receptive to those parts and to observe them in a more relaxed way. This alternation of elements on a small scale and areas on a larger scale provides a variation of attention that is absolutely indispensable.

Last, since these areas are often those in which one moves from one place to another, one may bring to the garden a very dynamic quality by creating rhythms, rhythms that accord, of course, with

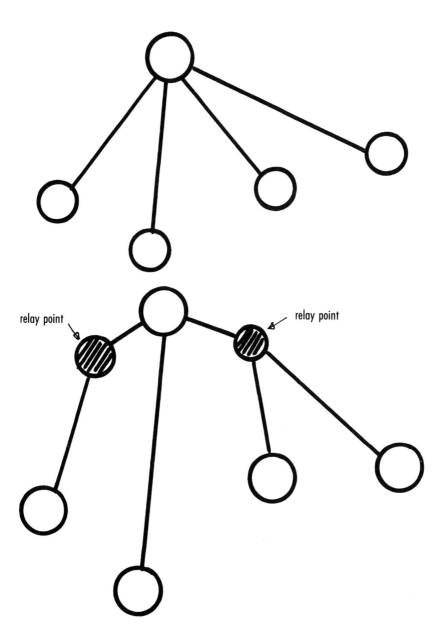

Fig. 6.   When too many views are available from the same spot,
we may replace our view by a relay point.

the nature of the movement required. Indeed, these rhythms may be solely visual and in no way lose their dynamism.

Though it is not necessarily so, one often sees these intermediary areas occupied by volumes:

—volumes created by the undulations of the site
—volumes created by fairly dense vegetation

Indeed, just as the points of interest must attract our attention, these volumes are designed in order to move it on, helped in this by the scale with which they are treated.

d. The sketch

The most important part of the work has now been done. All that remains is to give real shape to the ideas that have been assembled and correctly related to one another. In other words, we must now find the material representation of our ideas and wishes. This is fairly simple, provided the designer does not try to impose his own imagination, but, on the contrary, subjects it to the requirements of the plan that he now has before him.

It is at this stage that the style will really appear. Up till now, only the elements or constituent parts, the relations between them, and the areas accorded them have appeared. Their design was not yet important. This design will now appear, with its flowing curves, its lines, and its angles.

Let us take an example: a visual axis in a park may be materialized in different ways according to the style chosen (see fig. 7):

—a sinuous opening through the bushes, treated very freely
—a rectilinear expanse of grass emphasized by rows of compact masses on either side
—a rhythm created by a line of plants or an architectural rhythm (columns, statues, pergola, etc.), which will guide the eye along the visual axis
—a duality that will flank the view, punctuated at intervals, and emphasizing it—the axis of view passing to the center of this duality

For each element, for each relation, one must therefore find the appropriate materialization. But it is important to follow this procedure, and not the reverse.

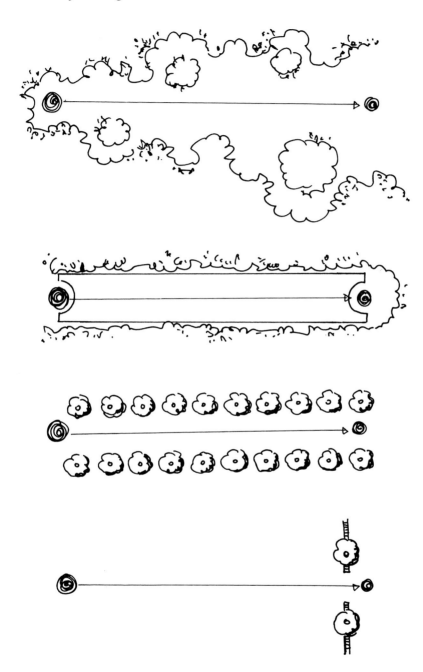

Fig. 7.   A visual axis in a park may be materialized in different
ways according to the style chosen.

The overall plan, then, is merely the graphic expression of the finished sketch and should illuminate everything that has been said up to now.

C. Applications

We shall now outline, in order to give concrete form to the method of composition that we have delineated, a series of five projects.

We shall presuppose that all the work described up till now—the analysis of the elements of the terrain (section I.A.1) and of needs (section I.A.2)—has been done, with the exception of the formulation of needs, or the organigram (section I.A.2.c), knowledge of which is necessary in understanding how projects are worked on.

Indeed, this earlier part, even though we have laid great stress on its importance, is not the real purpose of this book, which concerns above all a method of composition (chapter I) and a method of choosing plants (chapter II) for parks and gardens.

The five examples of projects presented here will begin, then, with the organigram and will end with the overall plan, with all the indispensable intermediary phases necessary to an understanding of the development of the project.

To sum up, each project will be discussed in five phases, corresponding to the preceding sections:

Phase 1.   The organigram (section I.A.2.c)
Phase 2.   Adaptation of the organigram to the site, or the general schema of organization (section I.B.1.)
Phase 3.   Plotting the areas (section I.B.2)
Phase 4.   Materialization of the elements and of the relations between them: The sketch (section I.B.2.d)
Phase 5.   The overall plan

The colors and numbers used in the projects correspond to the hierarchization imposed on the various constituent parts (the use of the colors varies noticeably in each series of plans, according to what is required, as there is sometimes a need for more than just the four colors alone):

—Red indicates the most important parts (sometimes numbered 1 and 2) and the fundamental relations.

—Blue indicates less important parts (3, 4, 5) and less important relations.

—Green indicates even less important parts (3, 4, 5) and less important relations.

—Yellow indicates parts incidental to the composition (4, 5, 6, 7) and quite unimportant relations.

Letters express the nature of the relations between the various constituent parts:

c = relation of circulatory movement
v = visual relation
a = relation of activity
p = relation of protection

Other types of relations might be found, and this list is intended merely as an example and is in no way exhaustive.

According to their thickness, arrows show the importance and privileged direction of each relation.

A commentary accompanies each phase in the various projects, but it is obvious that an attentive examination of the plans will explain the choices proposed better than detailed discussion.

1. First Project

This project concerns a small private garden of a very common type, situated in a residential complex, on the immediate outskirts of a small town in western France: a small site, an older, attractive house, neighborhoods quite near in every direction except the north, which has an interesting view. The family consists of two parents and three children (ages 15, 12, and 8). Both parents work (middle management), are very fond of their home, and like to entertain in a modest way.

a. Phase 1: The organigram

The needs expressed by the client are extremely limited and traditional: a terrace, lawn, utility area (for drying clothes, storing logs, etc.), flowers.

The suggestions made by the landscape gardener concern access to the garden (separate pedestrian and vehicular access) and a reception area, situated immediately in front of the house.

There are relations between these different elements:

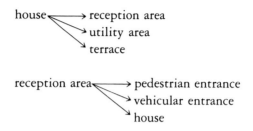

garage (in the house) → vehicular entrance

Thanks to the number of relations that it possesses with the other elements, we can now see the important role played by the so often neglected reception area.

A certain hierarchization, which might be modified at a later stage, is beginning to emerge:

        reception area → ①
        terrace → ①
        lawn → ②
        entrances, vehicular and pedestrian → ③
        utility area → ④

(See fig. 8.)

b. Phase 2: Adaptation of the organigram to the site, or the general schema of organization

In addition to the functional needs expressed in the organigram, there will now emerge elements deriving from the site that will make their own contribution to the personality of the garden.

    —the terrace: the orientation and plan of the house will split this up into three parts:

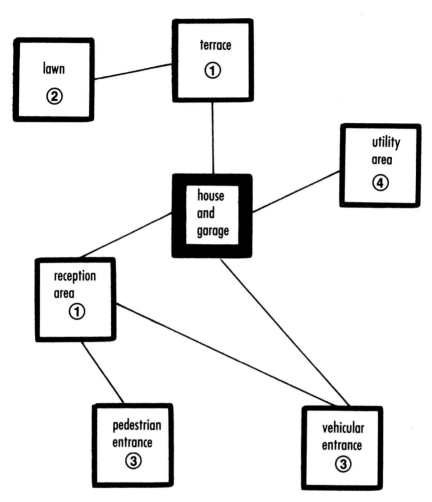

Fig. 8.   First project: phase 1, the organigram.

1. a south-facing terrace (in red, 1), which we will call the sitting-room terrace. It is well orientated, but rather exposed; we shall therefore protect it with screens (in yellow, 5) from the street and accesses (in green, 3)
2. another, north-facing terrace, the bedrooms terrace (in red, 1), not well orientated, but looking out over the most interesting part of the site: the lawn (in blue, 2) and the view (in blue, 2)
3. a third terrace, also north-facing, more relaxation area than terrace (in blue, 2)

The other elements already existing in the organigram remain in place, but their hierarchization is sometimes altered:

—reception area $\rightarrow$ 1 (in red)
—lawn $\rightarrow$ 2 (in blue)

Additional, but not very important relations are created that will facilitate communication between garden and house.

—Garage $\rightarrow$ sitting-room terrace $\rightarrow$ reception area $\rightarrow$ bedrooms terrace $\rightarrow$ relaxation area $\rightarrow$ utility area

The other relations develop very little compared with what was done in the organigram. We also find:

—a relation of circulatory movement (c) and a visual relation (v) in red, and therefore very important, between the bedrooms terrace and the relaxation-area terrace
—a relation of circulatory movement (c) and of activity (a) in blue, and therefore less important, between the relaxation-area terrace and the utility area
—a relation of circulatory movement (c) and a visual relation (v) between the relaxation-area terrace and the lawn, in blue
—a visual relation (v) in blue, between the lawn and the view

(See fig. 9.)

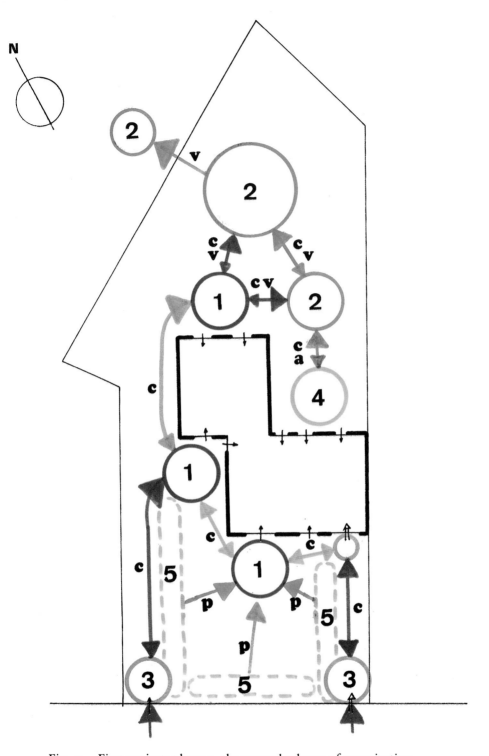

Fig. 9.   First project: phase 2, the general schema of organization.

c. Phase 3: Plotting the areas

Depending on their function, the various elements envisaged in phase 2 will now be accorded areas of varying sizes, various degrees of precision, various degrees of openness, etc.

Between these areas will be spaces that we will be able to plant, landscape, or leave in free, unbroken surfaces, but that will be treated on a slightly different (broader) scale than the one used for the elements in the strict sense.

Here the lawn, a fairly large area, will open out onto the interesting view to the north, which precludes any large-scale planting in that direction. The bedrooms terrace and the relaxation-area terrace also lead out onto the lawn, while the utility area will be turned back towards the house. The sitting-room terrace will open rather towards the pedestrian-access side, while being protected in three directions. The small reception area is connected only to the paths that lead into it. Colored patches will be placed on the three terraces and on the reception area.

(See fig. 10.)

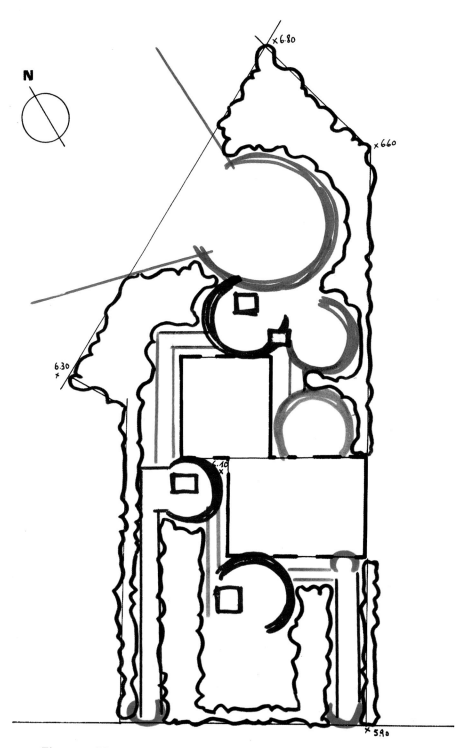

Fig. 10.   First project: phase 3, plotting the areas.

d. Phase 4: Materialization of the elements and of the relations between them— the sketch

Here the areas will take shape, the soil will determine how they are covered, the volumes specify their nature and siting.

—The sitting-room terrace, bedrooms terrace, and paths will be orthogonal in outline because of the shape of the house and the smallness of the site. They will be paved (terraces) or graveled (paths).

—The sitting-room terrace will be more fluid, more verdant, but with firm lines.

—The lawn will be surrounded in a very fluid way by "informal" vegetation.

—The colored areas will take the form of small square beds set in the terraces and borders along the blind gable ends of the house (flower beds).

—The plantings will be fairly limited, consisting of clumps of shrubs and isolated trees, with rows of informal low bushes serving as hedges.

(See fig. 11.)

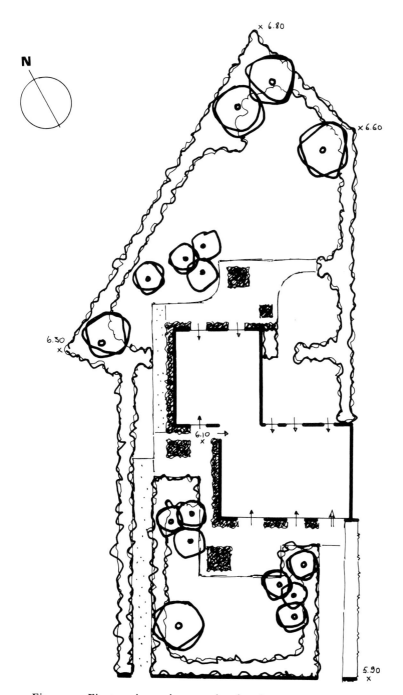

N

× 6.80

× 6.60

6.30
×

6.10
×

5.90
×

Fig. 11.   First project: phase 4, the sketch.

e. Phase 5: The overall plan

The design leads us to give greater detail and a final form to the contents of the sketch.

Here, for so simple a project, the names of the plants and materials have been shown on the overall plan, there being no need for technical plans indicating types of soil and plants.

(See fig. 12.)

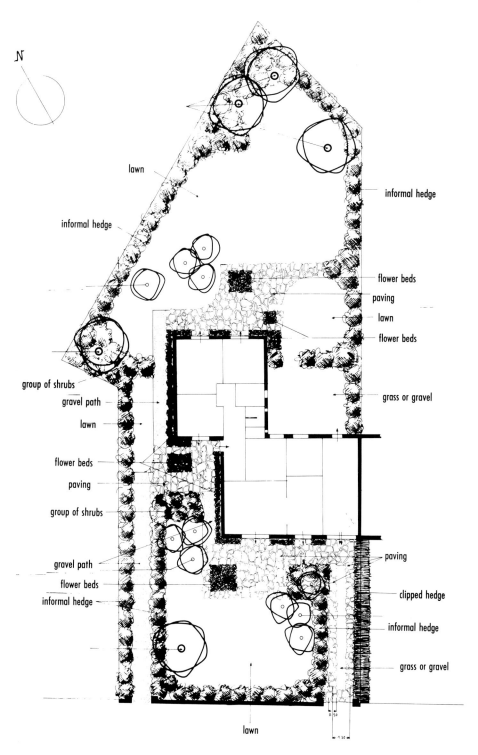

N

lawn

informal hedge

informal hedge

flower beds

paving

lawn

flower beds

group of shrubs

gravel path

grass or gravel

lawn

flower beds

paving

group of shrubs

gravel path

flower beds

informal hedge

paving

clipped hedge

informal hedge

grass or gravel

0 50

1 50

lawn

Fig. 12.   First project: phase 5, the overall plan.

2. Second Project

This project is for a fairly large garden, situated in the undulating agricultural countryside of the west of France. The house is old, of a type typical in the region, with huge outbuildings that are to serve as garage, workshops, stables, playrooms, etc. There are fine views to the south, east, and west, especially to the east and south. From the west comes the prevailing wind of the region. The family are local industrialists. The two children (ages twenty and sixteen) will soon be independent. The family like this area for its tranquil beauty and want their property to merge discreetly into the landscape. Riding horses is their favorite relaxation, and to the north there is enough additional land to accommodate a future paddock and exercise field. They like gardening, providing it is not too demanding. As for the style of garden, they would like something with an "old-world" character, providing it is not too exuberant.

a. Phase 1: The organigram

The clients' needs are fairly precise: a terrace adjoining the south side of the house, a shaded relaxation area, a sunny relaxation area, a modest orchard, a track leading to the ground kept for exercising the horses and to the road (north).

The landscape gardener suggests separating the entrances to the property: a service entrance (horses, delivery vans, tractors, etc.) and a main entrance, with parking for visitors.

The relations, which we shall not list here but which can be seen on the plan, show that, in this project, the important role is played, not by the house, but by the area between it, the garage-stable building, the parking area, and the service entrance.

On the other hand, the most interesting elements (see the hierarchization on the plan) are displaced in relation to this area.

(See fig. 13.)

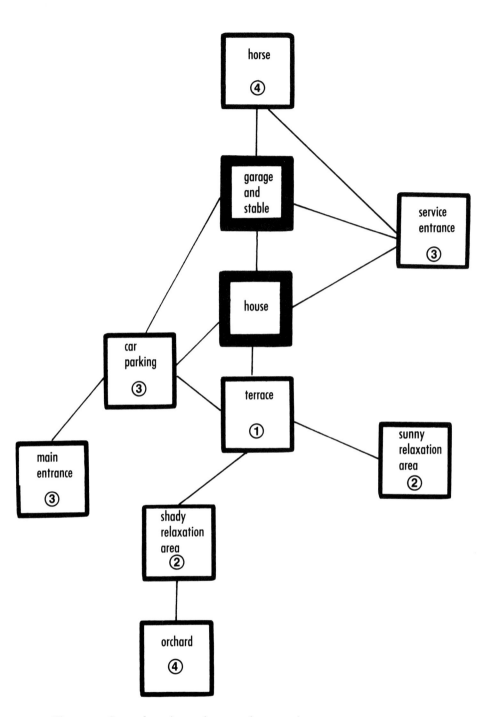

Fig. 13.   Second project: phase 1, the organigram.

b. Phase 2: Adaptation of the organigram to the site, or the general schema of organization

The elements contributed by the site and the personality of the client are now added to those envisaged in the organigram.

—Protective volumes (in yellow, 7) will shelter the southern part (orchard, relaxation areas) and the northern part (courtyard).
—There is a damp, marshy area at the foot of the former bakehouse (springs). It should be possible to incorporate water into the design here (in blue, 2).
—The sunny relaxation area (in green, 4) will be enhanced by this aquatic element.
—The shady relaxation area (in blue, 2) will be enhanced by the proximity of the orchard (in yellow, 6).
—Two views, to the south and to the east (in blue, 3), will be kept, in relation to the terrace, the shaded relaxation area, and the sunny relaxation area. The third view, to the west, is sacrificed in order to provide a windbreak.
—Finally, the area between the house and the garage-stable building obviously becomes a concourse for the traffic between the various elements in the property (in blue, 3).

Relations—whether important or incidental—of a different kind (circulatory relations, visual relations, relations of activity, and of protection) link the different elements, complementing those already provided in the organigram, as we can see in fig. 14.

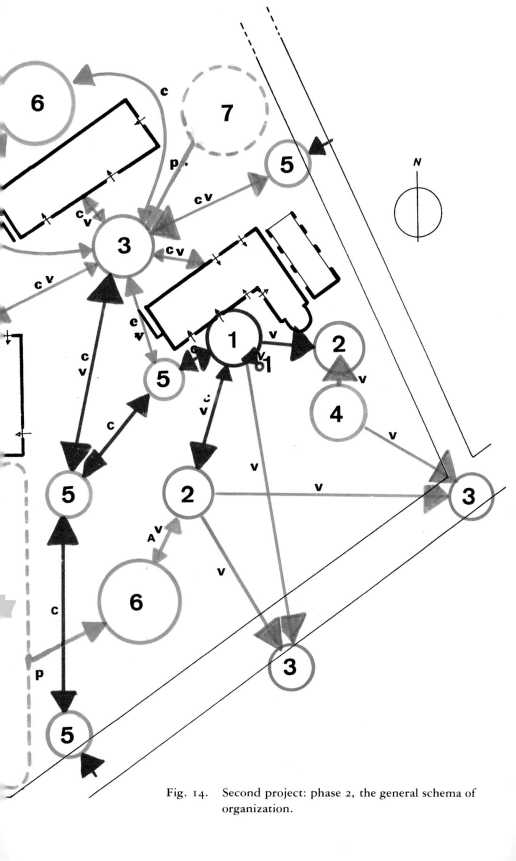

Fig. 14. Second project: phase 2, the general schema of organization.

c. Phase 3: Plotting the areas

In this project, it is above all the views that will plot the areas required by the client's specific wishes. These views will take the form of three conical "corridors" looking out, beyond the property, separated by volumes, in such a way as to avoid a single panoramic, uninteresting view.

The areas designated for relaxation will be differentiated: the sunny relaxation area will be larger, more open, and the shaded relaxation area will be smaller, more enclosed.

The courtyard, to the north, will have its real functional area (circulation) limited to a broad outer path, and the center left free.

The volumes, here exclusively plantings, will occupy the rest of the space, the orchard forming part of these planted volumes.

(See fig. 15.)

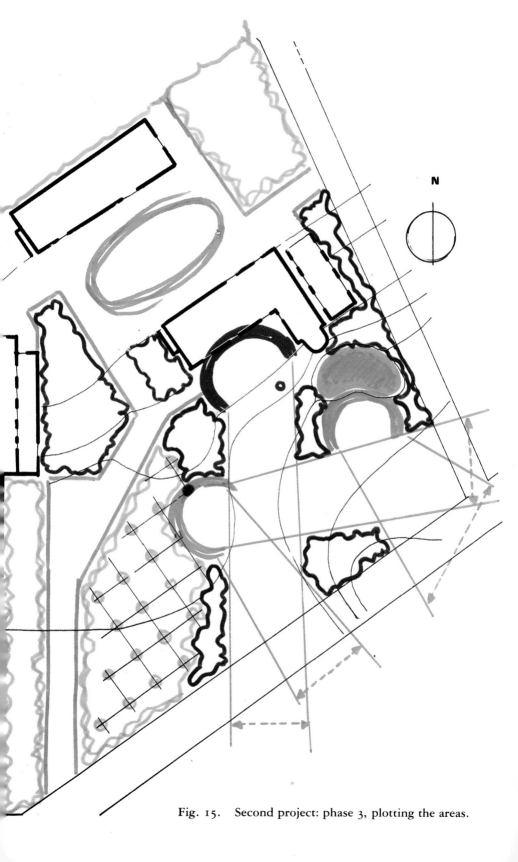

N

Fig. 15. Second project: phase 3, plotting the areas.

d. Phase 4: Materialization of the elements and of the relations between them— the sketch
The different areas take shape:

—The courtyard assumes a classical appearance, with grass and surrounding buildings. This is the form best suited to its function, to the oldness of the buildings, and to the tastes of its owners.

—The shaded relaxation area becomes a pergola, closely linked to the orchard, thus providing a transition between the orchard and the rest of the garden.

—The sunny relaxation area, on the other hand, becomes very "free," very vegetal, and not very clearly defined on the site. Its entire value resides in its closeness to the element below.

—The aquatic area becomes a pond, whose outline follows that of the bakehouse, and which will be accompanied by a whole range of plants suggesting water.

—The terrace takes on a severe form, well suited to the house, overlooking the site.

—The planted volumes will become a row (to the east, to accompany the path), a shrubbery (to the northwest, to enhance the courtyard), avenues (orchard), or specimen shrubs and trees (for purely ornamental purposes).

(See fig. 16.)

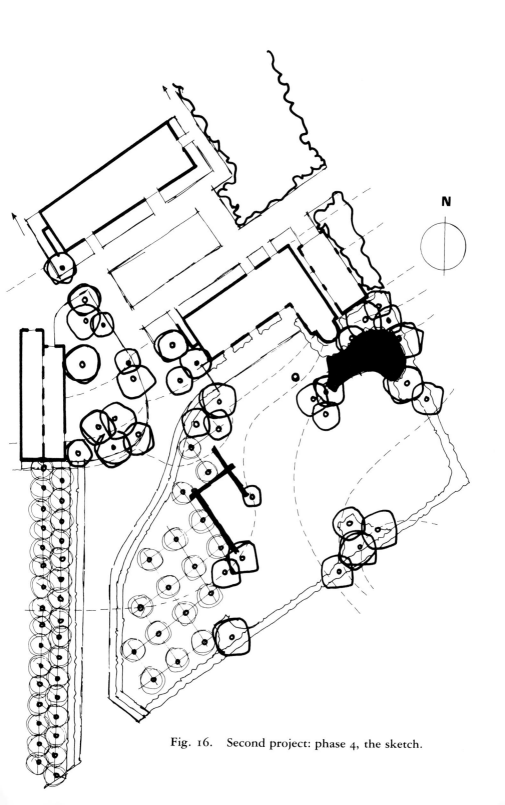

N

Fig. 16.   Second project: phase 4, the sketch.

e. Phase 5: The overall plan

The overall plan provides the detail and brings together everything planned in the earlier stages.

Here too, this being a relatively simple project, information concerning the soil and plantings are included in the overall plan.

(See fig. 17.)

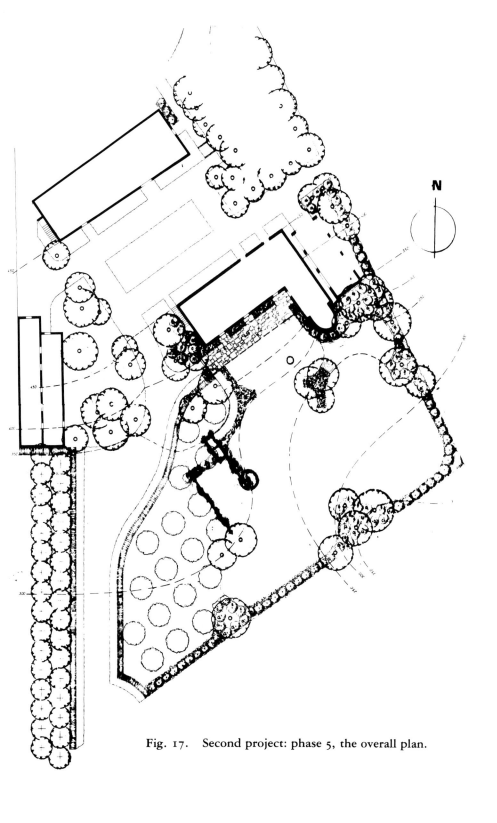

Fig. 17. Second project: phase 5, the overall plan.

3. Third Project

This is for shared gardens belonging to a complex of low-rise, fairly expensive dwellings, in a district on the outskirts of a town. To the southeast there is a bypass; to the northwest, a very busy street. Although the other two side streets, to the northeast and the southwest, are wide, they are quiet. Fairly near these dwellings is a good-sized sportsfield and a public swimming bath.

a. Phase 1: The organigram

Even though the space to be designed is a collective one, the needs expressed by the client are, once again, fairly limited: an area for children's games, an area for sitting, an area for walks, a sports area for teenagers and adults (perhaps a tennis court), an enclosure for the entire area, and above all, a very decorative element, intended to project a "brand image" that will impress the visitor (a suggestion advanced by the advertisers).

The landscape gardener suggests a separation between vehicular and pedestrian circulations and a meeting place, centrally located and easily accessible in order to make it a focus of activity.

It goes without saying that the service and safety equipment (fire-fighting equipment, garbage disposal, maintenance), have not been forgotten, but they must fit in with the other elements.

Similarly, we shall not go into the quantification of needs in terms of the number of residents, since this book is not concerned with the detailed working out of a program, and in any case, there is a regular flow of studies on this subject.

The relations depicted on the plan show the importance of the space between the dwellings and the value accorded the meeting place, a sort of turntable of activities, which we have therefore placed first in the hierarchy.

(See fig. 18.)

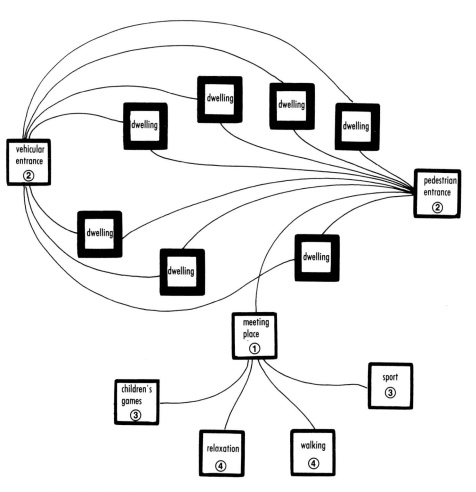

Fig. 18.   Third project: phase 1, the organigram.

b. Phase 2: Adaptation of the organigram to the site, or the general schema of organization

The site—its orientation and its environment—will add new data to the organigram:

—Access to the gardens will be from the quiet streets to the southwest and northeast (in blue, 2).

—Effective barriers (in yellow, 6) will be set up against undesirable factors (noise, view, danger) from the street to the northwest, and still more from the bypass to the southeast.

—These barriers, especially that to the southeast, will serve as a visual background to the meeting place.

—The "prestige" element demanded by the client will be placed in the important space already referred to, between the dwellings (in red, 1). It will be closely linked, both visually and in terms of circulation, with the meeting place (in red, 1). Between them, these two very important elements will form the "spinal column" of the gardens.

—The entrances to the buildings: the vehicular entrances (in green, 3), but still more the pedestrian entrances (in blue, 2), must be treated as an important point of interest in view of their continuous functional role. They will be placed in important relationships (both visually and in terms of circulation, in blue) with the prestige element.

(See fig. 19.)

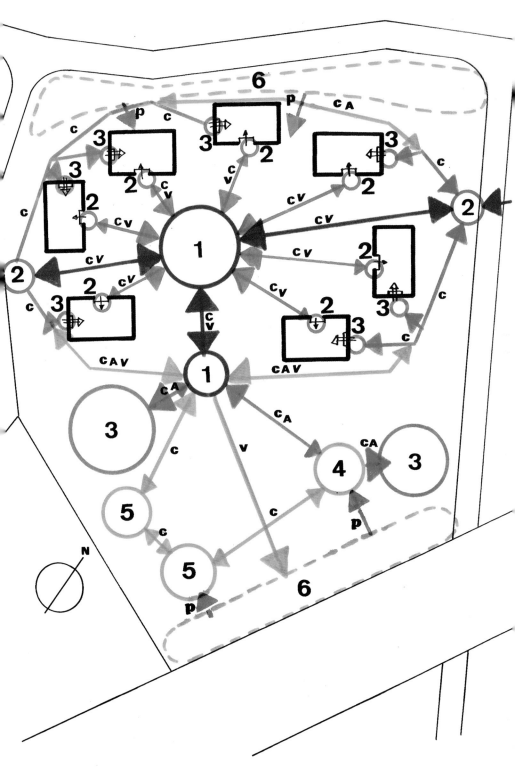

Fig. 19. Third project: phase 2, the general schema of organization.

c. Phase 3: Plotting the areas

Each element will be given a different area according to its needs:

—the central area, between the buildings, will be based entirely on the prestige element demanded by the client. In order to emphasize this effect, a design at ground level will radiate outward from this prestige element. Though this effect may be barely apparent to the pedestrian, at ground level, it will assume its full impact when seen from the windows and balconies of the dwellings.

—children's games will occupy a fairly large space, so as to be able to include different kinds of equipment.

—the spaces for relaxation, on the other hand, will be rather more limited in area, in order to preserve a sense of intimacy.

—the volumes (provided by different ground levels or by vegetation) will occupy the interstitial spaces, thus creating the enclosure, the barriers from the roads, the intermediary and background places that lend intimacy to the relaxation areas.

(See fig. 20.)

d. Phase 4: Materialization of the elements and of the relations between them— the sketch

As in the preceding examples, the sketch must now enable us to specify the forms, lines, and volumes of the design, and to decide what elements are to be included in it.

—The prestige element will consist of a highly architectural complex of pool, flower beds, and grassed areas at differ-

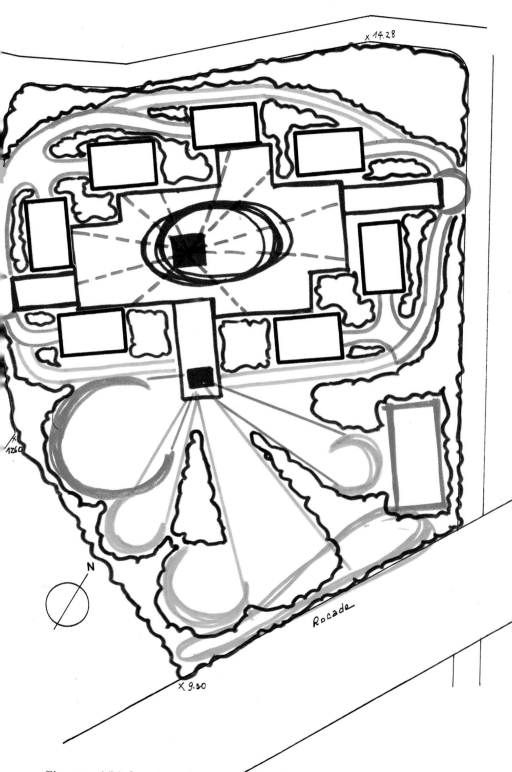

Fig. 20. Third project: phase 3, plotting the areas.

ent heights. The rest of the surface will be paved, and a design in the paving (natural paving stones of different colors) will converge on the pool, which will be the focal point of the complex. The complex as a whole will be designed to be seen by the pedestrian as well as from the dwellings themselves.

—The meeting place will be a stepped area, where teenagers might like to sit and chat, surmounted by a roof supported by pillars, thus providing protection against rain or sun.

—Between these two elements, the very strong link referred to earlier is materialized by a very long flower bed, similar to the beds around the central pool, and is flanked by two paths.

—The pedestrian access to the gardens will be treated in the same spirit.

—The children's play area will consist of a large expanse of sand, flanked in a very balanced way by two hillocks. On this sand and on these hillocks the games equipment will be installed. A path moving between the hillocks and the sand will serve as a circuit (bicycles, roller skating, etc.).

—The relaxation areas will consist simply of planted enclaves, linked by a path.

—The third relaxation area will be devoted to tennis, complete with a clubhouse.

—Finally, The driveways reserved for fire services lead into the driveways that serve the buildings, but certain differences (slight differences of level, different kinds of surface, etc.) will prevent cars from making use of them, and thus will make other activities possible (walking, bicycling, games of various kinds: hopscotch, ball, etc.).

—The volumes are of two kinds:

1. fairly sharp reliefs near the bypass (as a barrier against noise, etc.).
2. dense plantings of shrubs on the boundary (enclosure, protections of various kinds) and individually or in clumps.

(See fig. 21.)

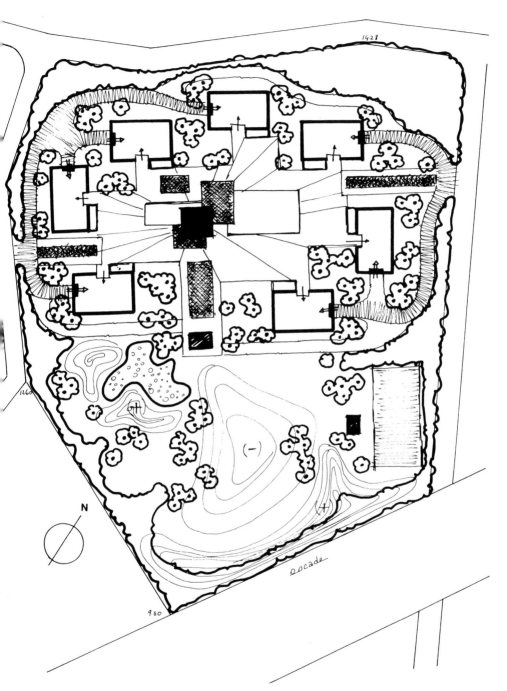

Fig. 21. Third project: phase 4, the sketch.

e. Phase 5: The overall plan

This carries the sketch a stage further. But this particular project, which does not concern a private garden as the previous projects did, and which is much larger and more complex, must be complemented by all the ancillary technical plans (concerning the planting, ground level, drainage, etc.) on an adequate scale.

(See fig. 22.)

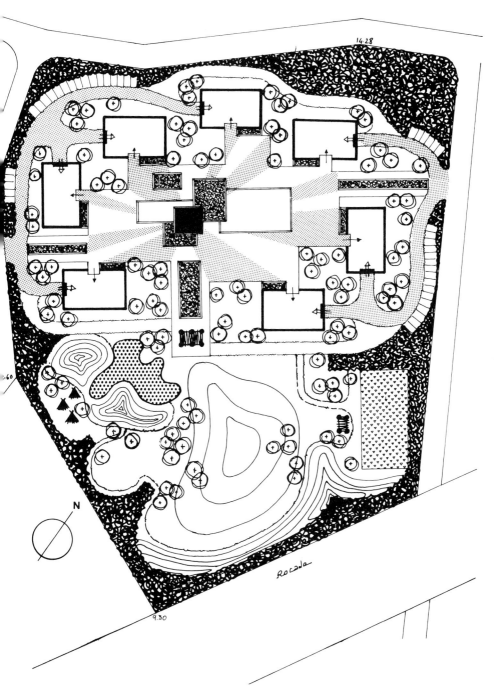

Fig. 22.   Third project: phase 5, the overall plan.

4. Fourth Project

This is a project for a private garden for a property in the Vendée, a region in France noted for its mixed woodland and pastureland: the house is of a style typical in the region, very low, very large, looking as if it has grown out of its terrace. At the outset the house had not yet been built, and it would have to blend in with an old farmhouse that had been converted into garages, games rooms, and workshops. The site to be designed, the boundaries of which had not yet been laid down for the landscape gardener except on the eastern side, extended through fields and copses to provide a most pleasing view. To the east, in fact, a driveway in very good condition led to the old farmhouse and, because it had to be preserved along the greatest possible length, set certain constraints. Like his wife and their grown-up children, the owner, a manager in an industrial concern, was fond of country life. For them, their home represented a haven of peace and quiet, the ability to keep animals, and a place to entertain like-minded friends.

a. Phase 1: The organigram

The needs expressed by the client were few, but precise: a lake, a large lake, as is often to be found in the region, irregularly shaped and bordered by already existing oak trees (the lake could be used for fishing and boating; one would be able to walk around it fairly easily, and it might have an island in it); a small kitchen garden-orchard, comprising a few trees, a few beds for cut flowers, an herb garden, a strawberry bed; a lot of flowers and flowering shrubs, for the garden must be very colorful (a gardener will be entrusted with its upkeep!); a small, very enclosed terrace-garden just outside the drawing room.

The landscape gardener added his own suggestions: install a pontoon, and an isthmus might be preferable to the much more common island.

There are not many owners of properties of this size who express no desire for sports facilities, but simply wish to enjoy the beauty of their surroundings.

(See fig. 23.)

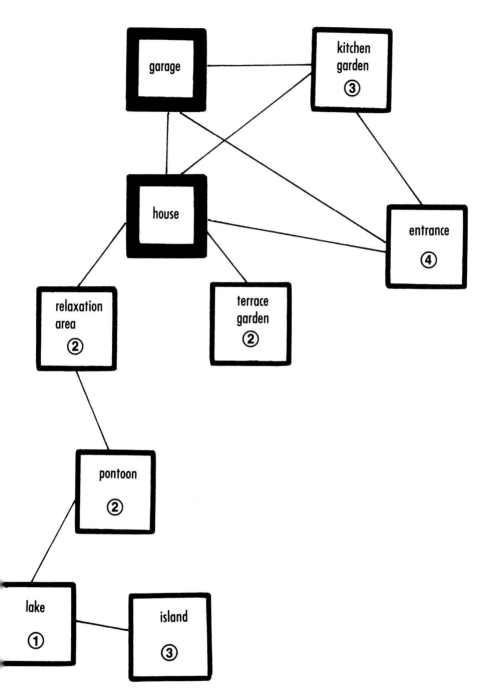

Fig. 23. Fourth project: phase 1, the organigram.

b. Phase 2: Adaptation of the organigram to the site, or the general schema of organization

The quality of the site, with all its possibilities, will enable us to have a very general schema of organization, despite a rather poor organigram at the outset.

—The lake will gain in importance if it is shaped in such a way as to divide it into three parts (in red, 1). The isthmus (in green, 3) will interrupt the outline, while making it possible to preserve a row of very fine oak trees. The pontoon (in blue, 2) will facilitate fishing, canoeing, or, quite simply, contemplation.

—The relative dispositions of the house and outbuildings necessitate two successive courtyards:

1. the first (in yellow, 4), directly connected to the entrance to the property (in green, 3), leads to the garage, while providing parking for cars and space for various activities associated with the gardener's workshop;

2. the second (in red, 1), the forecourt for the house itself, will be impressive and welcoming.

—Interesting views over the fields and surrounding landscape (in yellow, 5) deserve to be preserved, and in order to make the most of them, they will be broken up by masses (in yellow, 6), which will also serve as a barrier and enclosure.

—There will be relaxation areas, reached by paths, close to the flowers and shrubs envisaged:

1. a terrace-garden (in blue, 2)

2. a relaxation area in immediate proximity to the house (in blue, 2)

3. a relaxation area situated near the lake (in green, 3)

—Finally, the kitchen garden-orchard (in green, 3) finds its logical, practical place to the north, behind the outbuildings.

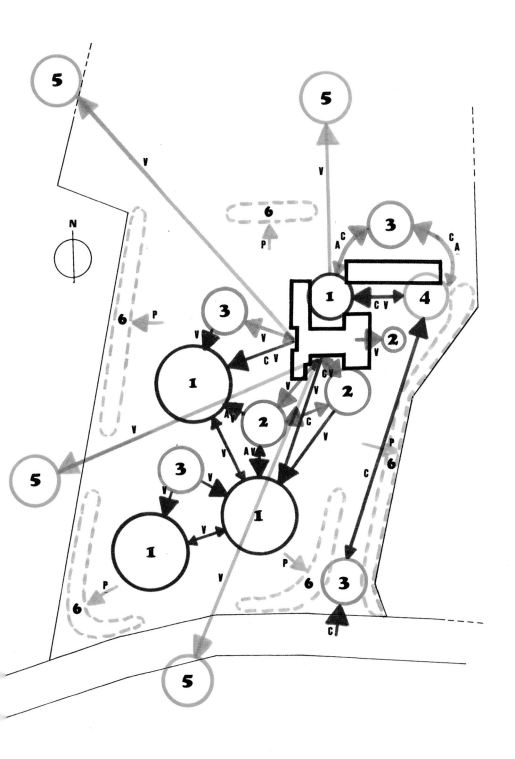

Fig. 24. Fourth project: phase 2, the general schema of organization.

The relations, as we see, gravitate around two principal poles:

1.   the house: the relations with the lake, the views, the re-laxation areas, and the entrances to the property.
2.   the lake: all (or almost all) the relations converge there, which explains why it is given the first place in our hierarchization.

(See fig. 24.)

c. Phase 3: Plotting the areas

Without saying too much about the other areas, which are similar to those in the earlier projects, something more might be said about the lake. It actualy occupies the major part of the site, leaving only a relatively small esplanade to the south of the house. The lake is the focal point of the garden and must be allowed to be as large as possible, with due regard to the already existing trees. The rest of the garden will merely be a transition toward the surrounding landscape. This transition will be achieved through the volume, relief, and planting elements.

(See fig. 25.)

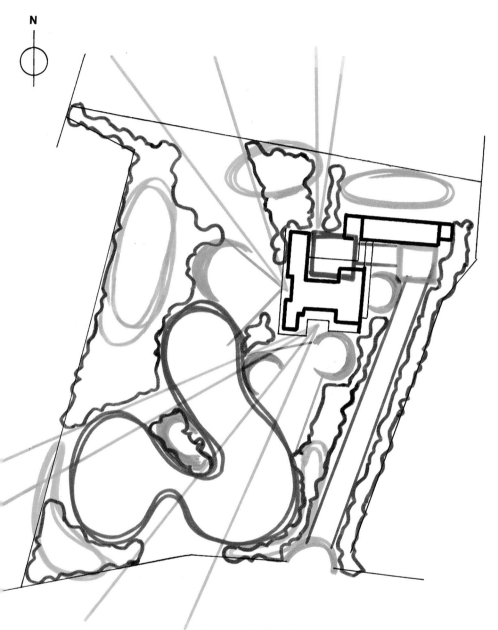

Fig. 25. Fourth project: phase 3, plotting the areas.

d. Phase 4: Materialization of the elements and of the relations between them— the sketch

Here we find the forms assumed by the lake, the driveway, the courtyards, and the walks, as well as the masses created by the reliefs and plantings, leading the eye towards the views beyond.

The relaxation areas assume their position in relation to the decorative plantings, and the kitchen garden-orchard assumes its final proportions.

(See fig. 26.)

N

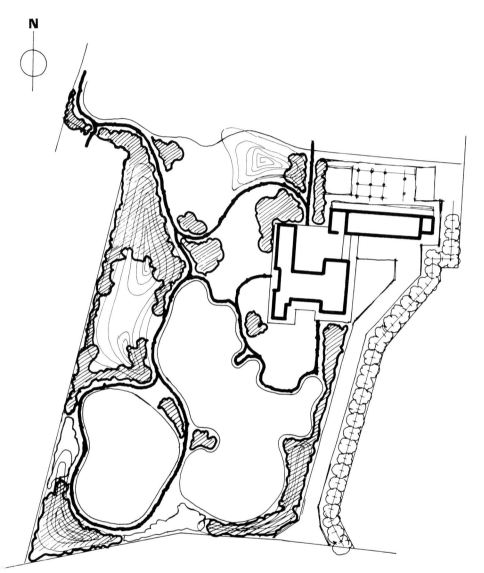

Fig. 26.   Fourth project: phase 4, the sketch.

e. Phase 5: The overall plan

The final design incorporates the specific wishes of the landscape gardener.

This project involves technical plans, in particular for the ground levels (the digging of the lake and alterations in levels) and the plantings, which will be fairly abundant.

(See fig. 27.)

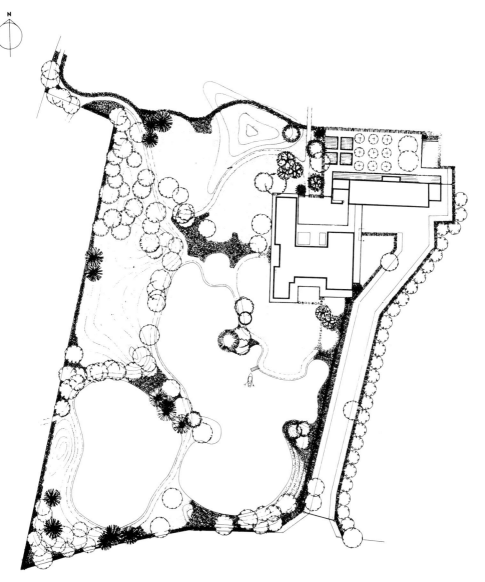

Fig. 27. Fourth project: phase 5, the overall plan.

5. Fifth Project

This project involves a historical reconstitution: not a restoration, for nothing existed here previously, but a return to a style that its owner prefers to any other.

The very large site slopes fairly steeply down to a marshy, easily flooded area and a stream. It is already wooded on its western side. It is bordered to the east by a road.

The owner wants to build a house, which will serve above all as a hunting lodge for the winter and will therefore not be very large. On the other hand, he wants a classical, formal garden. A great lover of trees, he wants to extend the existing woods for timber production (provision to be made for outbuildings, for this purpose) and to install an arboretum of conifers and hardwood trees. He wants to be able to walk around this arboretum and examine its contents.

a. Phase 1: The organigram

The needs expressed by the client were for a house (hunting lodge), outbuildings, woodlands for timber production, an arboretum, walks, and relaxation areas.

Suggestions made by the landscape gardener included a lake, in order to use the lower, marshy, easily flooded end of the site; an imposing entrance, worthy of the whole complex; and a terrace, which would increase the importance of the house.

(See fig. 28.)

b. Phase 2: Adaptation of the organigram to the site, or the general schema of organization

This project will be completely shaped by the characteristics of the site: the direction of the slope and the orientation of the site.

These two characteristics immediately determine:

—the part of the site on which the house is to be built (the higher part of the site)
—the orientation of the principal facade of the building (to the south)
—the area of access and reception (the northern part of the site)

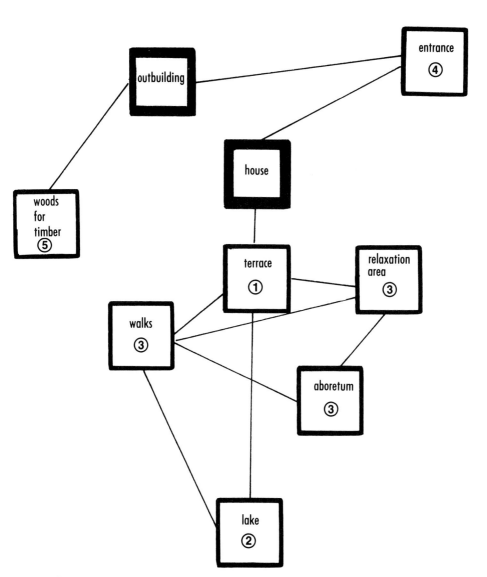

Fig. 28.   Fifth project: phase 1, the organigram.

There are three interesting views:

1. a fairly narrow but very beautiful one towards the south-southwest (in blue, 4)
2. a more open one to the southeast (in blue, 4)
3. a very specific one to the east-southeast (in yellow, 6)

These three views will be used to decide the exact position of the house. In fact, their axes intersect at a point that will be regarded as a key to the composition (in red, 2), commanding the focal point of the composition, which is the house (in red, 1).

But the axis governing the position of the house will not in itself be any of the three views. That will be another axis, the bisector of the two views represented in blue (4), which will terminate at a very important and closer point of interest (in red, 2), situated in a lake.

Around point of interest 1, the house, gravitate a number of elements envisaged in or added to the program—pools (in red, 2), gardens for walking in and relaxation (in blue, 3), and outbuildings (in yellow, 6)—the relations between these elements forming a geometrical shape.

In the woodland area, clearings (in yellow, 6) have been made in order to facilitate, during walks, a visual relation with the point of interest (in red, 2) situated in the lake, and therefore to enhance it.

(See fig. 29.)

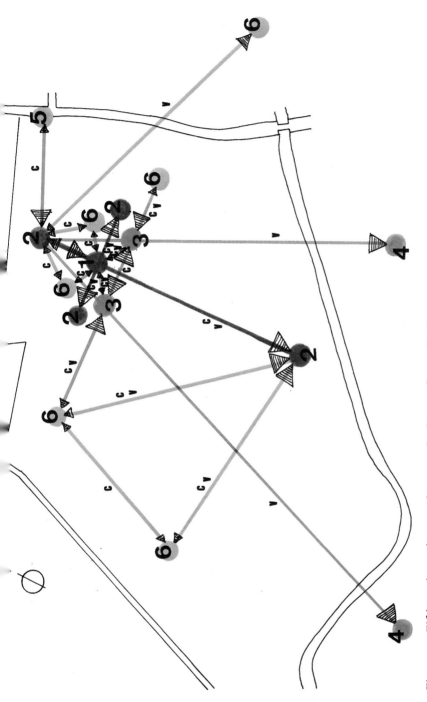

Fig. 29. Fifth project: phase 2, the general schema of organization.

c. Phase 3: Plotting the areas

We must decide which spaces are to be left without vegetation, or at least without tall vegetation (the slope allows the eye to pass over plants that are not too tall and situated at the bottom of the site, beyond the area to be designed as a garden proper). These are the spaces that correspond to the lines of sight—which are free to a greater or lesser degree, depending on the case—and to the other axes.

The elements on either side of the house will occupy areas that enable them to remain in the correct proportions to the house itself (whose visual importance, it should be remembered, has been increased by its terrace).

The lake will occupy the whole of the area subject to flooding in periods of high water. On the other hand, the strong point represented in red (no. 2) will be a mere point (but very attractive), as will the other strong point in red (no. 2), referred to above as the key to the composition and situated at the other end of the axis.

The volume of the plantings will occupy the rest of the site, providing a setting or border for the garden proper.

(See fig. 30.)

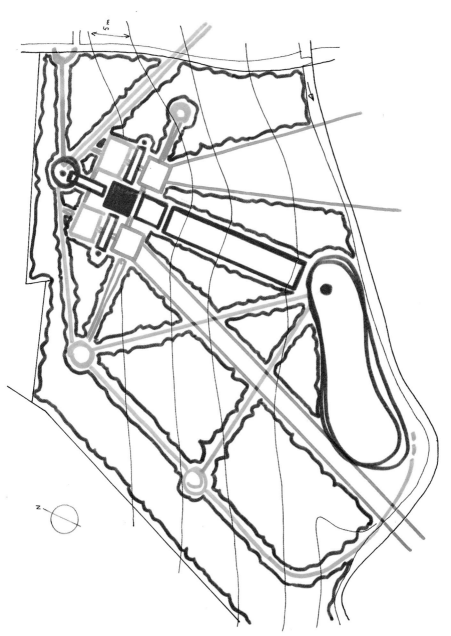

Fig. 30.   Fifth project: phase 3, plotting the areas.

d. Phase 4: Materialization of the elements and of the relations between them—the sketch

The areas plotted in the preceding plan will now take on their forms, and the elements that have not yet been decided upon will be identified and incorporated into the sketch.

—The space between the house and the lake, along the principal axis, will take the form of a green carpet descending in regular steps (leveling work to be carried out) towards the lake.

—The other part of this principal axis, to the north, between the house and the key to the composition (which may be a "crossroads" marked by a boundary post, a statue, etc.) will also take the form of a green carpet, but it will be much narrower. On the other hand, its rigor will be emphasized by an avenue of trees that will broaden out toward the house, but will extend along the driveway to the road.

—The arboretum will flank the two important views, thus providing a transition between the gardens proper and the surrounding landscape on view. It will also flank the green carpet.

—The formal gardens, the pools, and the terraces will, of course, involve great attention to detail, since their interest largely depends on the differences of level between them.

(See fig. 31.)

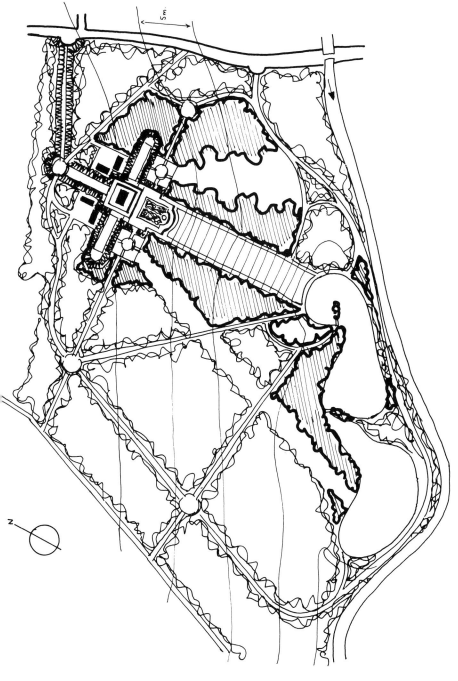

Fig. 31. Fifth project: phase 4, the sketch.

e. Phase 5: The overall plan

As in the previous projects, this stage provides the detail necessary for a full understanding of the entire complex.

Technical plans and a considerable amount of detailed information are indispensable to such a project of course.

(See fig. 32.)

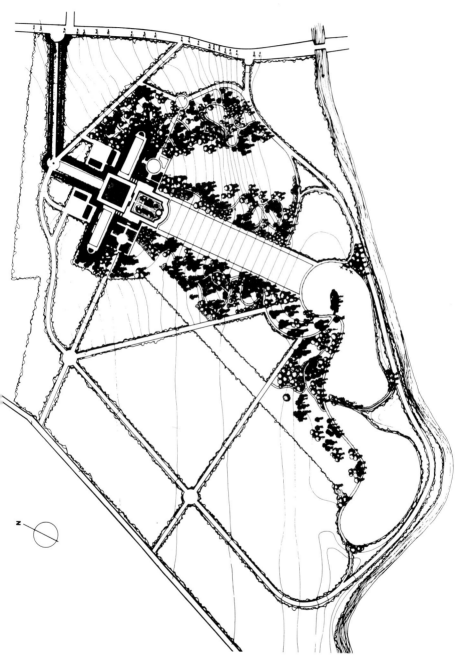

Fig. 32. Fifth project: phase 5, the overall plan.

II. The Plants

The problem of the use of plants may be summed up in two questions:

1. Which plants should be used?
2. Where should these plants be planted?

But one cannot approach these questions until one has previously answered others:

—For whom are the plants intended?
—What needs are being fulfilled by the plants?
—Where and in what conditions are the plants to be planted?
—What effect is being aimed at?

When posed in these terms, the problem is the same that faces any designer. It does not, however, stress the specificity of plants.

Plants are living things. They come in a wide variety of species and appearances. They are beautiful in themselves, so much so that the aesthetic aspect of a garden, which is based above all on plants, often has precedence over its functional aspect. They bear a heavy charge of subjective values, which make a logical approach to their use difficult, for "it's all a matter of taste," and, of course, *de gustibus non disputandum*. In many cases this attitude has given rise to "anything, anyhow, anywhere."

Figure 33 shows the interactions between the different parameters referred to above and gives some idea of their importance. It explains the approach that we have followed in this section, by dealing with the functions of the plantings, the types of plantings, and the choice of plants—taking into account the user and the design concept adopted, and never forgetting those numerous aspects of plants that make them such a unique material to work with.

A. The Functions of the Plantings

How is one to plant? Much of the answer will arise of its own accord if we have already addressed the question "Why plant and where?"—if, in other words, we have defined the functions that the plantings envisaged are supposed to carry out.

We will then have indications as to their precise siting, their volumes, their shapes, their densities, and their general appearance.

We are dealing, then, with precise functions, consequences of the program and the design concept adopted for the space in question, and not with the role of plants in general (whether physiological, climatic, psychological, sociological, etc.), which has usually no direct influence on a particular project.

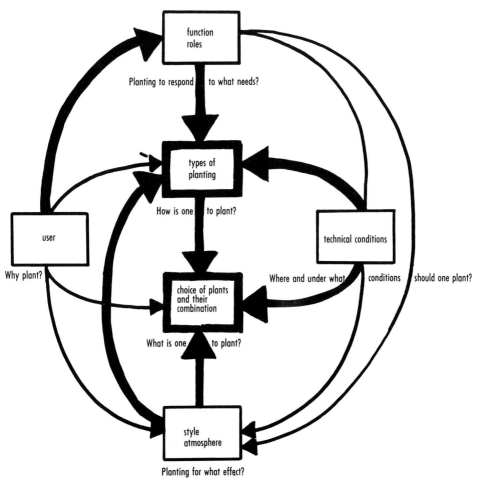

Fig. 33.   Aspects of the use of plants.

Fig. 34.   Plantings may be used as a visual screen, a windbreak, a
barrier against the sun, a sound barrier . . .

Since the term *function* is perhaps too vague and covers too
many different things, we have been led to break the concept down
into three types of functions:

1.   the utilitarian function
2.   the function of accompaniment
3.   the aesthetic function

1. The Utilitarian Function
This is usually the most easy to define, because, on the
one hand, it is fairly obvious to understand, since it concerns material problems, and on the other, because it is a consequence of the
program and of the existing state of the site.

It is not always very "noble" and does not necessarily deserve
to be emphasized. Examples of such use are:

—a visual screen
—a windbreak
—a barrier against the sun
—a sound barrier (see fig. 34)

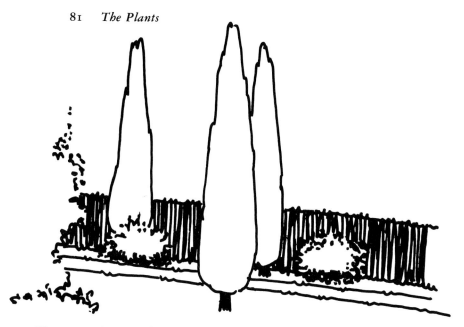

Fig. 35.   Plantings for enclosure.

—an enclosure (see fig. 35)
—a separation between two spaces (see fig. 36)
—a retaining wall on a terraced slope
—a covering for a piece of land

It is because there has not been an adequate analysis of the other functions that this function, which, as we have already said, is so obvious, often assumes a visual importance that it ought not to have.

The best example is that of overdecorative hedges whose only functional purpose is to enclose a space. The function of separation then assumes an excessive visual importance.

We should not go to the opposite extreme, however; to minimize their impact does not mean to forget them, but to make them unobtrusive.

2. The Function of Accompaniment

The function of accompaniment is to enhance, to emphasize, to reinforce, to minimize, etc.

In some cases, plants play the leading role; in others, they are

Fig. 36. Plantings used to separate two spaces.

secondary, but they are always subordinated to another element, which they serve.

We believe that this notion of accompaniment is of the utmost importance, a consequence of the rule of unity. It expresses a relation of dependence with regard to another element. It is neither of a utilitarian nature, for it may be quite gratuitous, nor of an aesthetic

Fig. 37. The use of a mass of vegetation to accompany the gable of a building that requires further emphasis.

nature, for that is not its primary role. Nonetheless, it excludes neither function.

Let us take an example. When we choose to use a mass of vegetation to accompany the gable of a building that requires further emphasis, we will have precise indications as to the siting, the shape, the height, the nature of these plants. Conversely—and it is perhaps even more important that this be understood—plants placed near a house have every chance of being perceived by the observer as dependent on it (fig. 37).

We have taken the example of a house, but it is obvious that this function may be applied to all kinds of elements: to driveways and walks (fig. 38); to various constructions—low walls, steps, pergolas, pools (fig. 39); to axes (fig. 40); to cross-axes; etc.

Plants have, then (as we shall see), a quite variable importance: as the accompaniment, or "garnish" one might say, to a building, or as a basic element serving to structure the composition (as is the case with cross-axes).

3. The Aesthetic or Decorative Function

This is perhaps the most important function, or in any case, it is the one most readily perceived by the public. They may

Fig. 38.   Plants accompanying a path.

Fig. 39.   Plants accompanying steps.

Fig. 40.   Plants accompanying an axis.

regard it as of such primary importance that it tends to conceal the other two functions—often so completely that one may wonder whether the landscape gardener has not forgotten them, along with the program.

The decorative function appears, therefore, as either an end in itself or a secondary aspect.

In landscape parks, for example—created for relaxation, walking, contemplation—the compositions, which are largely of a vegetal kind, often belong to the first category. In such cases plants must create: volumes and plans (fig. 41), backgrounds, splashes of color, contrasts, etc. in order to form scenes whose sole purpose is to please the eye.

When the decorative function appears as a secondary aspect, one tries to make one or both of the other two functions decorative (fig. 42).

Our modern parks and gardens—whose vegetation must serve as a windbreak, as a screen from undesirable views, as a sound barrier; channel the circulation of vehicles and pedestrians; accompany

Fig. 41.   Plants must create volumes and planes.

Fig. 42.   Scenes whose purpose is to please the eye.

houses and the various elements chosen; emphasize the composition, and be decorative—fulfill a utilitarian role that is both accompanying and aesthetic: they are the best example of this.

A particular planting may have several functions; the design concept may stress one or another of them, and the effect achieved will accordingly be very different.

4. Example

Let us take the example of a road enbankment. The functions of the plantings that are to cover it will be:

—to prevent soil erosion (utilitarian function)

—to serve as an optical guide (utilitarian function)

—to emphasize the roadway (accompanying function)

—to serve as a transition with the surrounding landscape (accompanying function—or function of integration, which may be regarded as a form of the accompanying function)

—to serve as decoration for the benefit of the driver (decorative function).

The solutions may be the following:

1. Stress the roadway in order to enhance it. This solution was often used during the last century: the road, a symbol of progress, was flanked by rows of plane trees, poplars, beeches, etc.

   This solution is aesthetic for the driver and also serves as an optical guide. On the other hand, it does little to integrate the road with the surrounding terrain, does not solve the problem of soil erosion, and is dangerous for traffic (fig. 43).

2. Make the plantings serve as a transition with the surrounding terrain. This is a very ecological approach, in which one would use native plants, grouping them in such a way that they recall the associations of the terrain.

   This solution is aesthetic, may help to prevent soil erosion, provides an optical guide, and may still have the effect of emphasizing the road (fig. 44).

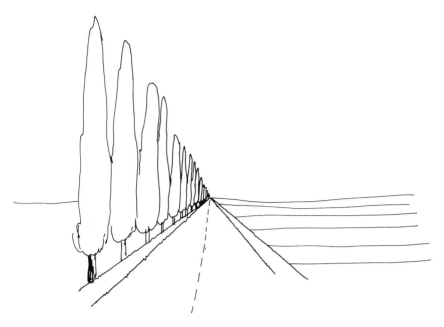

Fig. 43.   First solution: stress the roadway in order to enhance it.

Fig. 44.   Second solution: serve as a transition with the surrounding terrain.

Fig. 45. Fourth solution: be decorative.

3. Rapidly stabilize the soil. The best way to solve the problem, taking nothing else into consideration, is to plant grass or ground-cover plants.

Such a solution is not unaesthetic and depends a great deal on the context (the contour of the slope, the terrain, etc.).

4. Be decorative. Anything is possible if one does not take into account either the terrain or the road: from rock garden to rose beds (this is not unheard of!) (fig. 45).

These solutions show that not only are the aesthetic, logical planning, the utilitarian, etc., not necessarily incompatible, but, that on the contrary, these functions may reinforce and enhance one another. The decorative function invariably needs some material support. It follows that, in a project, any planting that has no other justification than to be beautiful must be suspect, and should probably be reinforced by or "harnessed" to some other function.

Similarly, planting as an "alibi" to hide mistakes should not be encouraged, for this constitutes, not a reinforcement of functions, but an obscuring of one by another. A fine slope does not necessarily have to be disguised as a rock garden; a fine building, well situated in its context, does not need to be smothered in greenery.

B. Types of Planting

Any planting, then, should be justified by one function or by several. It is important, therefore, to spend some time, at the outset, deciding which groups correspond best to the roles that have been defined. The actual choice of plants should take place only at a second stage.

Indeed, one does not decide to plant chestnut trees in front of a house without having thought about the way they will be arranged and the effect one is attempting to achieve.

Everyone knows the different types of planting, so, without describing them, we have set them out in the form of a table, together with their most obvious corresponding functions. Table 2 is a very general layout that may be extended in both scope and detail, but the important point here is the principle involved.

This type of table, with all its apparent limitations and rigidity, may give the impression that the landscape gardener's choice is severely limited. This is not at all the case, for—once one has decided on its functions—a shrubbery (to take a simple example) may then be treated in many different ways, by stressing: its design at ground level, its shape in space, its density, the way it is treated, the nature of the plants used, etc.

Although these possible variations have to take into account the technical conditions of installation and maintenance, the taste of the users, and of course the style and atmosphere aimed at in the design concept (see fig. 33), the possibilities of choice nevertheless remain very great, especially where plants are concerned.

C. The Choice of Plants

The choice of a plant involves a judgment, whether conscious or not, of its qualities and defects.

The importance of studying its technical characteristics seems

Table 2. Types of planting and their function

Type of planting	Utilitarian function	Subsidiary function	Aesthetic function
Tree or shrub in isolation	Create a point of interest Create a signal	Enhance a building Enhance some other element	Punctuate the design Create a foreground Create a reminder
Trees or shrubs in clumps	Create screens at certain points: visual screens sound barriers windbreaks	Enhance a building	Create successive planes Create volumes Creat effects of contrast and harmony (shapes, colors)
Avenue, row, clipped hedge	Create an optical guide Create a regular screen: a visual screen a sound barrier a windbreak Enclose a space Separate two spaces	Enhance a path Enhance a line Enhance an axis	Create a rhythm Stress an architectural effect Create a background
Unclipped hedges, lines of trees	Create a wide screen: a visual screen a sound barrier a windbreak Enclose a space	Provide a transition with the terrain	Create backgrounds Create green lines
Clumps of trees or shrubs	Provide a background for activities	Provide a transition with the terrain Create the effect of a border to stress a line	Create volumes Emphasize or reduce differences of level Create an atmosphere of vegetation Create backgrounds
Splashes of flowering plants (perennial plants, roses, bedding plants)		Emphasize a strong point	Create effects of color (contrasts and harmonies) and scent
Ground-cover plants	Stabilize the soil Cover unusable areas	Complement trees	Emphasize a particular atmosphere of vegetation
Grass	Stabilize the soil Cover areas intended for games, relaxation	Materialize visual axes, whether continuous or not	Enhance different levels and lines at ground level Create areas restful to the eye

obvious enough, but we are on more shaky ground when we try to arrive at a judgment of its aesthetic value.

Nevertheless, we have to go through both stages before we can approach the question of combining various plants, a question that, in itself, is a rather controversial one.

1. The Technical and Aesthetic Value of a Plant

a. Technical value

The technical value of a plant depends on a number of criteria concerning: its adaptation to the environment; its physiological characteristics of recovery, growth, etc.; its requirements from the point of view of maintenance; etc.

We have chosen not to deal with this fundamental aspect of the knowledge of a plant, since there are already a number of works on this subject. We shall confine ourselves to a few general remarks that might draw attention to a few sometimes neglected aspects.

—Adaptation to the environment:
In a particular, unaltered place, two types of plants may generally be planted: those whose range of use is restricted, and which are very characteristic of this environment; and those with a wider range of use, which may already exist in the terrain or may be introduced there. The temptation, for professionals, to develop the use of the latter is understandable, for they are polyvalent plants, which may therefore be produced in large quantities and are technically reliable because they are suitable to various kinds of soil.

The positive side of this attitude may be availability at low cost, an advantage that is often ignored by young designers. The negative side is a certain loss in "character," a certain repetitiveness in the choice of plants.

—Adaptation of the environment:
The opportunity to alter the soil, the microclimate, may be very positive, for it enables one to extend the range of usable plants. Unfortunately, it too is often a cause of repetitiveness, by making it possible to use the same plant in very different places. Need one give examples?

—Rapidity of growth:
This quality is becoming increasingly appreciated, and should therefore be taken into account. Indeed, present-day housing is built to last for a relatively short time, the road network is often being altered, and the users want to make use of the various installations at once. So we see the increasing use of rapidly growing plants, such as poplars, alders, and birches, which have a short life span.
—Maintenance:
Any additional difficulty in this area is expressed in increased cost. Certain qualities, which only a few years ago were regarded as of secondary importance, are now taken more seriously: resistance to destruction and vandalism, resistance to selective herbicides, the ability to cover ground rapidly (aggressiveness, competitiveness).

So one's knowledge of plants cannot be static. Our criteria of selection must be continually changing.

Every plant, then, has, in a sense, a technical "data card" that will assist us in deciding whether to reject it or keep it. But in most cases, even when the conditions of use are fairly restrictive, the choice of plants is determined primarily by their aesthetic qualities, and only later does one check that they are technically suitable.

b. Aesthetic value

When discussing the aesthetic interest of a plant, can one avoid such arbitrary judgments as "I love . . . ," "I hate . . ."?

It is often thought that any attempt to judge this aspect of a plant is doomed to failure, on the grounds that aesthetic judgments belong to the realm of subjectivity—the preserve of artists and impervious to reason.

By rejecting any analysis, this common negative attitude often leads to ignoring the most important aspect of a plant, or to being content with the superficial judgment mentioned above, whereby appreciation of the plant world is divided into two blocks, the "beautiful" and the "not beautiful."

And yet, it is an undeniable fact that a sequoiadendron has

greater visual impact than a willow, that the outline of cypress of Provence is more eye-catching than the less-marked one of a tamarisk.

Nevertheless, we may prefer the willow to the sequoiadendron and the tamarisk to the cypress.

Could it be, then, that there is an objective idea of a plant ("the objective plant") and a subjective idea ("the subjective plant")?

(1)   The "objective plant"

This could be defined as the sum of all the elements that may have a visual, olfactory, tactile, or gustatory effect on the observer.

In arriving at this judgment, one might use a sort of "checklist" that would enable one to take into account all the various interesting elements:

—size
—overall volume
—shape: fastigiate, slender, pyramidal, precision of outline
—foliage: texture, color, persistance, mobility, variation in
   time
—trunk: shape, texture, color, etc.
—branches: ditto
—flowering: duration, period, brightness, etc.
—fruit: decorative value, taste, duration, etc.
—odor
—sound produced
—exceptional characteristics that might have a bearing on
   the size or shape, the color of the leaves, fruit, branches,
   roots, etc.

The purpose of this exercise is, not to rank a plant on a scale of ten, but, by analyzing it objectively, to become aware that a particular plant is overvalued or undervalued. The kind of conclusion arrived at might be, for example, that plant x may be used in isolation, for by virtue of its shape, texture, and fruit, it will have sufficient aesthetic value; or again that the interest of this shrub lies, above all, in its globular, informal shape, and in its fine, gray-green foliage. It may therefore be used as a background.

We said, "may be used" advisedly. For us, then, such an analysis is a way of avoiding errors of judgment. It is sometimes interesting to apply this method of analysis to plants we are particularly fond of: we then realize that we have accorded them extra marks for subjective reasons of our own.

It is this latter element that we shall call the "subjective plant."

(2)   The "subjective plant"

We make this subjective judgment, usually in an unconscious way, by referring to a personal or collective system of values.

As we know, the tree is the bearer of a great many symbols: life, strength, longevity, paternity, etc. Certain species of tree—the oak, for example—embody these symbols in a special way; others in a more modest, more general way. Is there not an entire symbolic system conveyed in the language of flowers?

The ease with which we associate a particular plant with a known shape, a symbolic or artistic reference, reinforces its value, for it enables us to "identify" it. This is so in the case of plants with very marked shapes: conical, round, spreading, picturesque, etc.

These symbolic references may be innate or acquired, personal or collective.

History may increase the emotional power of certain plants. We have already mentioned the oak, because of its symbolic value; it also has a historical value, as does the olive, the yew, the laurel, the lily, etc. (fig. 46).

A plant belongs to a particular environment, whether natural or not, with which we try to associate it. If we have never seen it, we compare it with another plant whose origin we do know (just as a tourist abroad sees landscapes and towns that remind him of his own country). Thus, for many people, conifers, in all their variety, become quite simply "firs," and any tree of "weeping" habit is perceived as a weeping willow.

Plants, then, bring with them the particular atmosphere of the places with which we associate them: this atmosphere is more or less precise according to the geographical distributions and frequency of

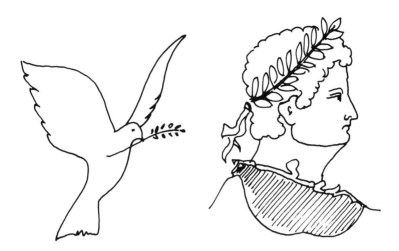

Fig. 46.   The olive has a historical value, as does the laurel.

appearance of this referential plant, which may be more or less strong, depending on the value of the terrain associated with it.

Using the same plants in all places—over and above the effect of saturation that it produces—makes them monotonous and deprives them of any "emotional message." The plant that used to suggest the seaside becomes "that plant next door."

Finally, a plant is often associated with an actual personal experience; some have a particular significance for us because they are linked with happy events in our lives, or with places like a garden we knew in childhood. This confers on them an emotional value that is often incomprehensible to others.

These personal references can only come into play, of course, when one is planning a garden for oneself, and may result in either originality or incongruity.

As we shall see, this system of references depends on the personality of the observer and on his family, social background, and age. It changes with time.

A number of practical applications may be derived from these observations:

1.   It is important that we should be able to differentiate, in the judgments we make, between collective references

and individual references, for only the first are usable when we are selecting plants for a public garden or park.

2.   We may divide plants into those that bear strong collective references, and have therefore an increased value, and those whose references are weak or few in number. The first will be less universally usable than the second, which are more neutral and therefore more polyvalent.

3.   It is important that the designer have a knowledge of the social group for whom the park or garden is intended, for it will influence his choice of plants.

We shall come back to these last two points when we approach the question of combining plants.

(3)   Conclusions

The study of functions enables us to define the types of planting to adopt. A study of plants enables us to assess their technical and aesthetic value and thus to determine whether a particular plant will be suited to the use for which it is being considered.

We have approached the subjective aspects of the problem with a view to isolating the "tastes" of the users and the contradictory reasons given for one's judgments.

This knowledge, in depth, of plants is indispensable to us when studying the combinations of plants, which involves technical knowledge but which aims above all to be decorative.

2. Combinations of Plants

The mere juxtaposition of plants, however beautiful, does not necessarily create a true combination. That presupposes something more, which might be expressed in the formula: "The combination of plants A and B produces something more than the sum of plants A + B," or by such terms as atmosphere or emotion, which the Japanese call *fusei*.

a. The mechanism of combination

The eye has a tendency to group together similar elements: this is what occurs when stars are grouped into constellations.

With dissimilar elements, the eye tries to find relationships, connections, with a view to achieving a coherent whole, a unity.

These connections may be alien to the plants themselves. In other words, it is the context in which they are used that creates the unity: for example, the use of relief, of visual line, of a particular material or element that frames them (fig. 47).

This is the case in those all too common groups of varied shrubs, which remind one of Jacques Prévert's "inventory": a for-

Fig. 47.   Dissimilar plants may be linked together by a particular material or element that frames them.

sythia, a veronica, a genista, and . . . a rhododendron. And yet such groupings "get by"—thanks to well-defined lines at ground level, perhaps, or the framing of a visually very strong paving (fig. 48). The eye is thus forced to link together plants that have no connection between them. If we take away the paving, the lines lose their clarity. The legibility disappears.

This way of using plants simply contributes variation, which may be pleasant enough but requires strong unity. This unity may be created by:

> —elements such as paving (mentioned above), low walls, paths (fig. 49), hedges, water, grass;
> —composition: we have already spoken of lines at ground level, but variations in the level of the ground, axes, rows of shrubs or trees, or the shaping of shrubs may play a similar role;
> —proximity: in order to form links between plants, they must be close together. In well-established parks and gardens,

Fig. 48.   Dissimilar plants may be linked by the framing of a visually very strong paving.

where the foliage of different trees and shrubs intermingle, the eye does not challenge the juxtaposition of the various elements. The overall design is apparent to all: one reads only a single mass of foliage. This explains why one must sometimes wait several years before one can understand the designer's intention: the link between two stalks planted ten meters from each other is not at all an obvious one. In fifty years, that link will exist, even if it was not very strong at the outset (like wine, gardens improve with age!).

The recent fashion in design takes this fact into account by planting more closely together, which makes the composition of the space more legible.

But when the landscape gardener—and this is usually the case—tries to find plants that are directly related or have common references, a true combination is created.

Before turning to the different types of combination available, we might sum up the different cases already mentioned, in terms of

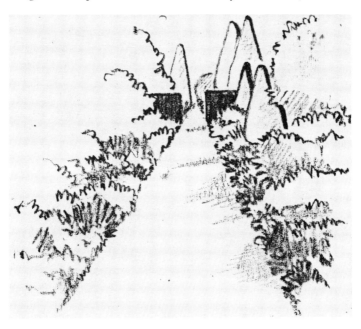

Fig. 49.   Elements such as paths may establish a visual relationship among dissimilar plants.

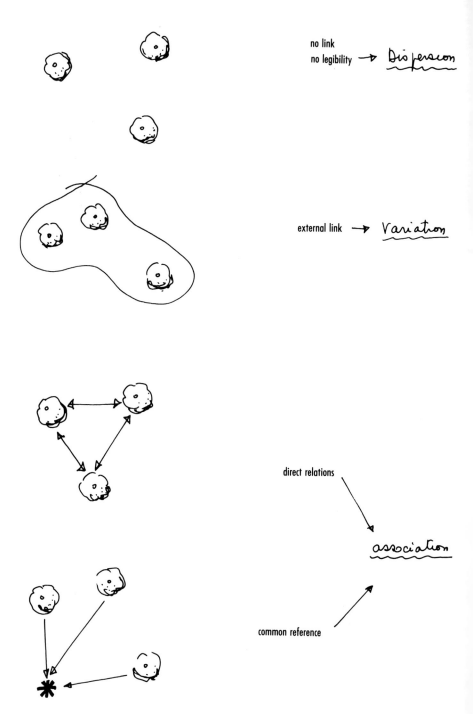

Fig. 50.   The different types of combination.

the schemata in figure 50: isolating the different types of connections will help us to gain a clear understanding of more complex combinations.

b. The different types of combination

(1)   Combinations of an ecological or natural type

Of all the references that plants may carry with them, one, by definition, recalls the combination of plants, and that is the reference to nature. Indeed, plants are always combined together in nature and, except in the case of cultures, seldom grow in isolation.

The "landscape" style derives from this fact; did it not aim from the outset, to imitate nature, in, among other things, its vegetation? And yet the use of plants gives rise to problems in designs based on this school. Without going over the entire history of landscape gardening, we should remember that, in the course of time, the imitation of nature became imitation of what was best in nature, and that of what was most extraordinary and most curious in it. So much so that, when the landscape gardeners had at their disposal all the marvelous exotic plants from every corner of the world, the beauty of the plant obscured the reasons for its use. Beauty was sought, not through combinations, or arrangements, but through the elements themselves.

However, when one shows a photograph of a fairly typical combination of plants to even a fairly wide public, it is usually identified and approved. We are in a situation, then, in which there is a very strong collective reference, applied this time, not to a single element, but to a set of elements, to a family of plants in the ecological sense of the term, which suggests a given environment.

This suggestive power is all the greater in that the effects reinforce one another, and a certain dynamism is created by the addition of partial references.

A willow may suggest water, but if it is combined with poplars, the reference becomes more precise (fig. 51); it will become still stronger if one adds alders, meadowsweets, water irises, and reeds. A whole family of plants will have been obtained.

Fig. 51.   A willow may suggest water, but if it is combined with
poplars, the reference becomes more precise.

These very legible, very typical families, with strong references—rock plants, dune plants, bog plants, etc.—are commonly
used in our gardens.

But garden arrangement is not ecology, and the faithful imitation of nature is not always technically possible or aesthetically desirable, and encourages neither creativity nor new ideas.

These ecological families must, then, serve as a basis to inspire
the creation of more open, less restrictive "landscape families," our
basic concept remaining, of course, the common reference to a particular environment.

To begin with, we shall be able to broaden it very easily, by
combining plants from similar environments, but very different re-
gions. When we visit the exotic garden at Monaco, for example,
where succulents from the arid zones of every continent grow side by

side, it does not occur to us to challenge these combinations, which strike us as quite obvious (fig. 52).

So we will be able to substitute plants of similar appearance, the untrained eye identifying the unknown plant introduced with some very common plant, or even confusing the two.

Cultivars easily replace well-known types of plant in this way—but similarly, the epicea can replace the fir; the astilbe, the meadowsweet; the fescue, the molinia; etc.

Certain plants, as we have seen, have several facets, and it is the plants that accompany them that bring these out.

The birch, combined with heathers, suggests damp moorland; combined with "firs," the skirt of a forest in a cold climate; combined with oak trees and chestnuts, a low copse under full-grown trees.

New Zealand flax, combined with dry rock plants, is related to

Fig. 52.   In the exotic garden at Monaco, succulents from the arid zones of every continent grow side by side.

Fig. 53. New Zealand flax, combined with dry rock plants, is related to yucca.

the yucca and the agave (fig. 53); beside water, it becomes a cousin of the iris (fig. 54).

Finally, many plants have no very precise references and are very polyvalent. This does not mean, however, that one can use them anywhere.

California privet, for example, is so widely used that one is no longer surprised to find it everywhere (at the seaside, as undergrowth, and in clipped form). However, used as a background to a dry rock garden, it will bring a note of incongruous greenness and freshness that will destroy the desired effect.

In order to illustrate this, let us take an example from an ecological family, and see how it has evolved as part of a landscape family.

Damp moorland is made up of plants of which the most typical are the following: *Erica tetralix*, *Ulex gallii*, *Molinia coerulea*, *Genista anglica*, *Salix repens*, *Carex*, *Sphagnum*, etc. To these may be added in

Fig. 54. New Zealand flax, beside water, becomes a cousin of the iris.

transitional zones with similar features: *Quercus robur, Quercus toza, Betula pubescens, Pinus sylvestris, Pinus pinaster, Salix cinerea, Erica cinerea, Erica ciliaris, Calluna vulgaris, Prunus spinosa,* etc.

At first, the landscape gardener will keep only those plants that interest him because they are decorative and have strong evocative power. The others—*Salix repens, Sphagnum, Prunus spinosa, Salix cinerea,* etc.—will be eliminated, since they add nothing.

Then we shall carry out a few substitutions and a few inversions in the relative importance of the plants: a wide variety of heathers (and not just *Calluna vulgaris*) may be used, and this will give us a more continuous and more varied flowering. The birch, a very important element, will be given special prominence, but the *Betula verrucosa* will replace the *Betula pubescens* because the soil in most of our parks and gardens is usually less favorable to the latter. Among the pines, *Pinus nigra* "Austriaca" will replace *Pinus sylvestris* and *Pinus pinaster,* for it is more easily found in nurseries, and more suitable to the soil, and it possesses greater powers of recovery. The *Pinus mugho nanus* (or some other form of dwarf pine) will recall either young pine seedlings or the picturesque dwarf forms that survive in extreme conditions. Broom will replace gorse, because it is easier to maintain, grows more rapidly, and possesses a variety of genera, species, and cultivars. We thus have a perfectly traditional family used very often in gardens, and one that appears to be very little different from the strictly ecological family.

But one may go farther: moving from plants that grow on acid sandy moorland to plants that grow in leaf mold, a whole new world of azaleas, rhododendrons, and andromedas opens up to us. One may wonder what justifies such an amalgam, apart from the technical conditions of the soil, but one then realizes that, in this particular case, the references are to be found in horticultural exhibitions, catalogs, and various gardening books.

This brings us to a phenomenon that is subjacent to visual references, namely, what the eye is used to. The eye creates its own references: it gets used to particular combinations. Referential landscapes may, then, be altered, for good or ill, in such a way that one gets used in the end to the ugly as well as the beautiful: the Eiffel Tower has become part of the national heritage, and in fifty years, there may even be a Society for the Protection of the Leyland Cypress, who knows?

So far we have only considered the use of natural scenic references—those, therefore, that are very descriptive in intention. The interest of this type of reference is not solely in the imitation of extraordinary landscapes, for that will be fairly limited. The method may be extended and applied to less precise references, such as to natural atmospheres.

In this case, the difficulty will be precisely to overcome this inherent vagueness, and therefore to define the atmosphere desired in such a way as to be able to make a coherent choice of plants. To define an atmosphere is not to say simply "I want luxuriant, natural, fresh vegetation," for on the basis of these three adjectives, one can find several families of relatively different plants: a mountain atmosphere, with plants like the spruces, firs, and larches; or a valley atmosphere, with poplars, alders, and willows; or a woodland atmosphere, with beeches, yews, and ivy; or a "rural" atmosphere, with beeches, elms, apple trees, and meadows.

It is clear that a mixture of all these plants would destroy the atmosphere that one might have set out to create initially.

The definition of atmosphere involves, then, a reference to a natural environment that is expressed in terms of the shapes, contours, masses, textures, colors, smells, sounds, etc., and also of the plants that are typical of that environment.

As we have seen, these references may be very widely used, so much so that it is sometimes difficult to free oneself of them. Do not irregular plantings—obeying no very legible utilitarian or accompanying function—make a reference to the natural?

(2)   Combinations by harmonies and contrasts

In this case, there is a direct reading, that is to say, the eye perceives the relations between the various elements presented to it: relations of similarity, in the case of harmonies; or relations of opposition, in the case of contrasts.

It is more the "objective plant" than the "subjective plant" that is taken into account in this type of combination, where the plant is regarded above all as a material.

Our first consideration will be to define the forms, volumes, colors, and textures of the plants that we wish to use, then, taking technical criteria into account, we shall have to decide which plants to use.

Here we shall not be describing scenes of vegetation, nor shall we be seeking inspiration in natural atmospheres; creation can therefore be entirely original. Constraints disappear, but so too does the safety not provided by reference to the natural.

Combinations through harmony lend themselves to the use of a large number of plants, which is not the case with contrasts. We will tend to use them to set up backgrounds, transitional areas, beds or groups of plants to accompany some other element—in short, everything that gives unity to the plantings, and therefore to the garden.

Very often, one will find harmonies of shape, color, material (foliage) combined together. Plants native to the Atlantic or semi-continental climates, most of which are deciduous, produce, by their vague outlines and the subtle texture of their foliage, harmony rather than contrast (fig. 55).

This is also the case with certain groups of plants that lend themselves particularly to monochrome combinations: perennial plants, often in delicate tints of blues, mauves, pinks, and yellows (fig. 56); mixed heathers, in carmine pink tints; graminacious ground cover in various green tones: gray-green, blue-green, golden green; conifers, also in a variety of greens; etc.

Fortunately, parks and gardens are, in themselves, despite the efforts of certain designers, monochromatic compositions of green.

Harmonies ought to be legible for most observers. In fact, the effect produced is often hardly noticed, because it is too subtle, or because it is regarded as insufficiently decorative by a public that prefers the stronger effects created by contrasts.

Whereas harmony creates a subtle atmosphere that will be perceived by the observer to a greater or lesser degree, the more dy-

Fig. 55.   Plants native to the Atlantic climates produce harmony rather than contrast.

namic element of contrast must arouse a reaction and therefore be more easily read.

The eye, as we have said, contrasts and therefore compares elements, which presupposes a relation of similarity between them, for one can only compare what is comparable. It is difficult to make a contrast out of two quite different elements. Many attempts to do so have failed because this fact has not been taken into account.

When the opposition concerns only one aspect of the plants brought into combination, the contrast is very legible, as, for example, with a bed of blue and yellow pansies. This legibility diminishes as variation increases. It is not easy to read a contrast between a purple maple and a Lawson's cypress, for the contrast operates

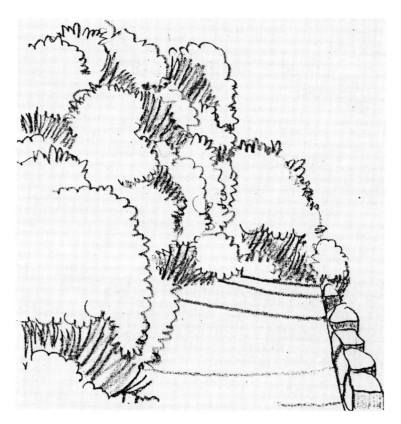

Fig. 56.   Perennial plants combine to produce harmony.

through color (deep purple and golden green), form (globular and slender), height, texture, etc. In other words, the two trees are not really comparable at all.

Plants are a complex material, so one seldom finds pure, and therefore perfectly legible, contrasts.

In formal gardens, which make great use of contrasts of shape, there is little variation in the texture of the foliage (yew, box, cypress), or in the color (a fairly limited range of greens), and the various shapes are stressed by pruning and topiary work (fig. 57).

Fig. 57.   Formal gardens make great use of contrasts of shape.

The cypress of Provence, an almost perfect vertical, is also clipped in order to reinforce the contrast it forms with the horizontal or globular elements in the garden (fig. 58).

Contrasts of foliage are subject to the same requirements, if one wants them to be legible. As we have seen, Atlantic plants do not easily lend themselves to contrast, and their combinations can yield only a fairly limited range of variation. On the other hand, Mediterranean and especially exotic plants provide contrasts not only of form but also of foliage. Tropical hothouses are a good example of this. Of course we are astonished by the rarity of the plants and their extraordinary size, but the combinations of foliage, which are often fortuitous, create extremely decorative effects.

The contrasts preferred by the general public are contrasts of color, which are largely a matter of flowers. However one should not forget the worthy effects of Pissaro's plum trees, Koster's spruces, Drummond's maple, etc., to set one another off over the last few decades.

One cannot conceive of a garden without colors: without flowers, it would be deprived of its best part. However, creating

Fig. 58.   The cypress of Provence contrasts with the horizontal or globular elements in the garden.

contrasts does not mean juxtaposing every possible color (gardens are like cakes: too much makes you sick). On the other hand, there are contrasts of color that are an aggression on the eye. Lack of legibility is then hardly the problem, for lack of any other qualities.

One must, of course, take into account the tastes of the users, and we have stressed the importance, for the landscape gardener, of knowing the public for whom his design is intended. A flower bed in front of a railway station cannot be the same if it were situated in front of some historic building. However, one often meets effects that are rather too facile.

(3)   Various references (other than ecological)

The two broad types of combination referred to above are very widely used, for they are addressed to a very large public. There are, of course, more limited references, such as those to the visual arts or to literature, and more esoteric references, such as those to symbolism or to religion. All these references are to the intellectual or emotional experience of the public; they are therefore perceived by each individual as very personal. They are interesting to use, for each individual who perceives them is under the impression that he alone is being addressed, he alone has noticed the reference.

Reference to painting is a very old practice: one has only to remember the origin of the term *paysagiste*, which, in the seventeenth century, referred to painters of landscapes and not to gardeners.

Of course, these paintings were inspired by nature, but we also know that the earliest romantic gardens were designed like paintings. Kent was a painter, Pope a writer, and Rousseau inspired the earliest French romantic gardens by his descriptions.

Writing, then, by its evocative power, may be a source of references.

The connections between buildings and gardens have, above all, been ever-shifting power relations, which have taken on different forms according to the style employed:

—subjection of vegetation in formal gardens, in the interests, above all, of contrasts between form and material: the green

columns of the trees correspond to the columns of the pal-
aces, hedges to walls and balustrades, harmonious couples
in which the mineral played the nobler part

—domination of vegetation in the landscape style, which tries
to integrate architecture, but often achieves no more than a
juxtaposition

—confrontation in certain modern gardens, where the contrasts between materials are very strong

In such a case, the vegetal is defined in relation to the
mineral, the garden in relation to the architecture, from
which it borrows a good many of its rules of composition
(contrasts, proportions, rhythms, etc.) (fig. 59).

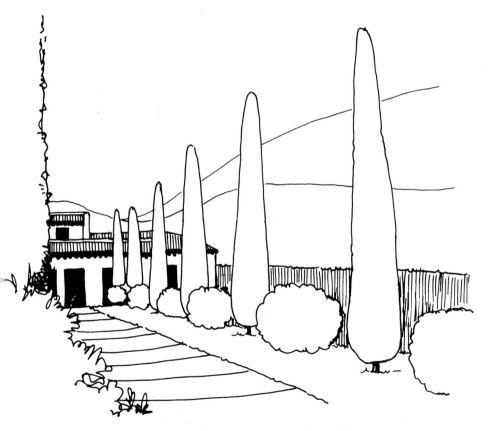

Fig. 59.   The vegetal is defined in relation to the architecture.

These various references (to painting, literature, historical gardens, architecture, etc.) are references to an intellectual experience, to personal reminiscences of reading, of traveling.

Emotional experience may also be a rich source of references. Let us take, for example, what is a very sentimental reference, powerful because it involves our childhood memories: our grandmothers' gardens. The atmosphere of that garden, whether recalled or rediscovered, will not fail to arouse in us a highly charged emotion, and moreover, each of us will believe that he is the only person in the world to feel it. The combination of plants that will give rise to this emotion might begin with the lime tree, often to be found in old-fashioned gardens, and lead on to a whole mass of trees, shrubs, and flowers, each of which conjures up potent memories: horse chestnut, hornbeam, lilac, flowering hawthorn, bay tree, hazel tree, various liburnums, cornel tree, hortensia, aucuba, spiraea, old roses, not to mention perennials such as phlox, blue iris, peonies, hollyhocks, asters, sweet williams, fuschias, columbines, and finally, the box hedges bordering the paths.

We have seen how the subjective value of plants has its origin in, among other things, symbols, but as far as Western gardens are concerned, symbolism stops there; it does not determine the combination of plants, as in Persian gardens (the combination of cypress and almond blossom symbolizes life and death) or in Japanese gardens, in which the entire design of the garden is based on symbolism.

Eden is a luxuriant garden that we tend to imagine as abundant in vegetation, inhabited by good-tempered animals (fig. 60). But does such an atmosphere, however precise it may be, provide us with any reference as far as the combination of plants is concerned? It may, and one may see it as a search for extraordinary, marvelous plants: this is apparent in the work of such naive painters as the Douanier Rousseau, with their exuberant, simplistic plants, combined in contrasting masses.

In moving from conscious symbolic reference to unconscious symbolic reference, one finds the "enchanted garden," of dream or fairy story. One imagines rustling plants (the ginko, bamboos), plants of surprising size (sequoiadendron giganteum), of twisted bearing (paulownia), of enormous leaves (catalpa and ailanthus

Fig. 60.   Eden is a luxuriant garden.

stumps, gunnera, certain magnolias with caducous foliage, large heracleums), strange colors (almost black purples, blues, dazzling golds), enormous (disturbing or marvelous) flowers with heavy scents, creeping lianas, carpets of moss, etc.

So there are many kinds of references, but the important thing is that the public to whom they are addressed be able to read them.

(4) Complex associations

In order to achieve a better understanding of the nature of the links between various groups of plants, we have had to isolate the relations and to render them schematic. But it is clear that, in most cases, the combinations of plants are complex and are the sum of the different types of links referred to above. This is inevitable, for, as we have seen, a simple relation exists only when the plant is very stylized, which is a fairly rare occurence.

The consequences of this may be unfortunate; the effects may cancel one another out. The reading may become more difficult as the number of references offered increases—or, on the other hand, the addition of effects may produce a richer, more powerful whole.

On the other hand, because the appreciation of the observer varies with what we have called his system of personal references, some observers will be more susceptible to the color of the composition, others to its forms or its evocative power.

Finally, plants are living organisms, and their appearance changes: there are gardens that are to be discovered in the morning, others in the evening; some should be seen in the spring, others with their autumn colors.

It is this richness that produces the originality of plants and makes their use so bewildering. If we go back, more prosaically, to our basic schemata, as in figure 33, we see how complicated these may become. Let us take a few cases.

1. The combination of the cypress of Provence and the holm-oak is a very strong one, for it conveys a very obvious reference to Mediterranean landscapes, supported by contrasts of form that may be still stronger if the cypress is clipped and the holm-oak particularly twisted; the contrast of material, on the other hand, is weak. Furthermore, they are very common plants; they may bear personal references as well as symbolic ones. Such a complex combination, therefore, is a very powerful one and not one to be repeated anywhere. (See fig. 61.)

2. Let us imagine a weeping willow and a group of water irises planted at the edge of a pond. These two extremely

Fig. 61. Cypress of Provence and holm oak.

well-known plants refer to the same environment, water, an environment that creates a very strong visual link. This combination is an obvious one, despite the absence of any direct relations between two plants that are so dissimilar as to produce no harmony or contrast whatsoever.

3. In a rock garden, the combination of fastigiate juniper and dwarf pine is perfectly acceptable. The juniper is quickly identified as a calcareous rock plant, the pine as a native of rocky mountain scree. The common reference to rock becomes obvious, especially when made explicit by the actual presence of rocks and sharp reliefs. The strength of the combination will be further stressed by the con-

Fig. 62.　What can we say of the combination of a fastigiate
juniper (*Juniperus communis* 'Hibernica') and a golden
prostrate juniper (*Juniperus chinensis* 'Pfitzeriana Aurea')
beside a pond?

trasts between the conical shape and the low, rounded
shape.

4.　What about a combination of the fastigiate juniper (*Juniperus communis* 'Hibernica') and another, low-growing
golden juniper (*Juniperus chinensis* 'Pfitzeriana aurea') beside a pond? They form an obvious contrast of forms, together with a variation in color. The first suggests dryness
by its shape and by the gray color of its foliage; the second, because of its universal use, has come to lack any
particular association. However, the combination is more
characteristic of hot, dry environments than damp ones.

And yet we have seen these two plants together beside ponds! There is certainly an acquired reference here (exhibitions, catalogs, magazines), or perhaps a wish to link two different environments (dry and wet) (fig. 62).

5. The combination of a bluish-leaved sheep's festule and a bluish-leaved hosta may be perceived in different ways: it is easy to read the contrasts of foliage between the two plants, as well as the harmonies in the blues. On the other hand, there is an antagonism between the two natural references: the first (the fescue) suggests dryness; the second, damp undergrowth on the water's edge. If one places this combination beside a pool, with a few pebbles, the eye will see the fescue as a water grass, in spite of its color, and the whole will seem coherent. But if one replaces water with sand (a dry stream), it will be difficult to see a blue-leafed hosta as a native of a dry environment, and the antagonism will persist.

We have taken a few simple examples, for of course, these schemata soon become illegible as one increases the number of plants and types of relations. The aim is not to show that plant combinations are complicated, but rather that they are open to reasoned analysis. What interests us, then, from our pedagogical point of view, is the extent to which these schemata exemplify certain analytical principles. When confronted with a group of plants, one has to ask oneself the following questions:

—What are the elements of coherence and variation?
—How are these elements to be perceived by the observer?

We would not like to end this section on the complex combinations of plants without saying something about certain mineral elements mentioned briefly above, which, when used in small quantities, are integrated by the eye as forming part of the plant family, or are associated directly in contrast with the plants surrounding them. Usually these elements have a certain evocative power and, by their presence, reveal the natural, symbolic, or artistic reference intended. Rocks, pebbles, gravel, sand, etc., are such elements.

c. Plant combinations and the composition as a whole

Plant combination does not form an independent entity, as we have already made clear.

The functions retained by the design concept, the style, and the atmosphere imply a type of planting to which the plant itself is subject; the potential user of the park or garden and the technical conditions of carrying out the plan have to be taken into account also. (See table 1.)

The coherence of the plantings largely depends on what we have called the external links, those created by the elements in the garden, but above all by the strength of the composition as expressed in the lines and forms.

Some people have believed that only a knowledge of plants was necessary to compose a garden, and that combinations of plants were sufficiently decorative in themselves not to require an overall design. This is the worst service that can be given to ornamental plants, for by making them an end in themselves, one justifies the opposite excess, which is to treat plants by the square meter and thus to deprive oneself of the infinite possibilities of combination offered by them.

D. Proposal of a Method

To sum up this section on the choice of plants, we would propose a method of work that may be carried out in five stages:

stage 1: precise definition of an atmosphere
stage 2: definition of the function of the different plantings
stage 3: choice of a basic plant
stage 4: choice of a "family" of plants
stage 5: final choice and siting of the plants

In order to illustrate this method and to make it concrete, we will go back to the second project used above in chapter I.

Let us turn to phase 4 in the development of that project, that is to say, to the phase referred as "the materialization of the elements and of the relations between them—the sketch." Indeed, the plants are an element in the garden, and we have seen how their approximate siting was begun in phase 3 ("plotting the areas"), and how in phase 4 ("the sketch"), their outline, volume, nature, density—in short, all their characteristics—then became more precise, as is the case for the other elements. But, as we have seen, the plant is an element quite different from the others and requires particular attention here in stage 4.

1. First Stage: Precise Definition of an Atmosphere

In section II.C.2.b.(1) we said something about the term *atmosphere*. Whatever solution is chosen (reference to a natural environment or an entirely artificial atmosphere), we must describe it in a very precise way, illustrate it with a descriptive vocabulary, imagine for ourselves the forms, colors, scents, shadows, feelings, and reminiscences that will suggest this atmosphere.

In the project under consideration, the tastes of the client, the style and age of the house and its dependencies, the nature of the landscape beyond the garden, all concur to give great importance to the particular rural nature of the terrain. We have therefore chosen an atmosphere that is inspired by it, and that we will characterize in the following way:

—The plants will have to create gentle harmonies of color, form, and material: the forms will tend to be rounded, the moving folige will give an impression of coolness, accentuated by the large areas of grass. The greens will be preferably fresh green, avoiding dark or golden greens.

—In order to emphasize this effect of coolness, the colors will be chosen predominantly from among the whites and pinks. We shall avoid violent reds, yellows, and oranges, as too warm, and blues and violets, which would be overpowered by all this greenery.

—We must not forget the style of the buildings and their age, or the taste of the residents for an "old-fashioned" but sober and elegant style.

—Finally, a slightly different atmosphere could be allowed in the area of the pond, with its natural springs; a still more verdant, more luxuriant atmosphere, suggesting the presence of water, might be sought, while remaining within the general atmosphere of the overall design.

2. Second Stage: Definition of the Functions of the Various Plantings

A study of the sketch (fig. 16) will enable us to define the types of planting (see section II.B), and therefore to work out the nature, density, decorative value, etc., to be given to the plantings.

If put directly onto the plan (see fig. 63), this study will enable us to see very quickly what should be altered, what cut out, and what further emphasized.

Let us turn back to the sketch and justify the functions to be carried out by our plantings. (See table 3.)

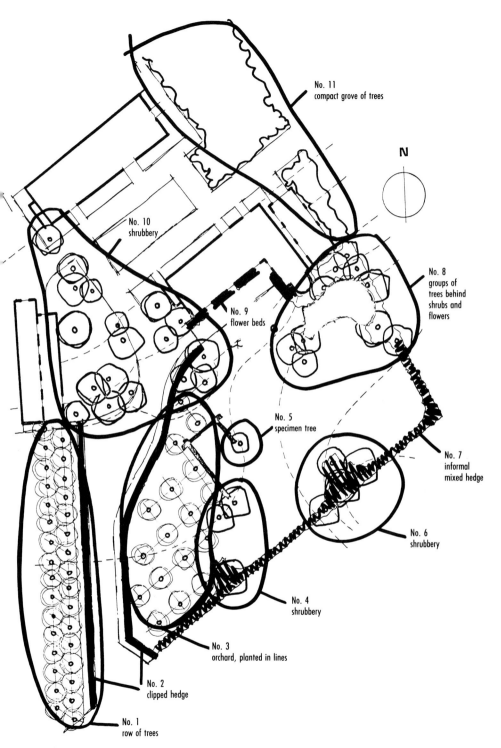

No. 11
compact grove of trees

N

No. 10
shrubbery

No. 8
groups of
trees behind
shrubs and
flowers

No. 9
flower beds

No. 5
specimen tree

No. 7
informal
mixed hedge

No. 6
shrubbery

No. 4
shrubbery

No. 3
orchard, planted in lines

No. 2
clipped hedge

No. 1
row of trees

Fig. 63.   Types of planting in the second project.

Table 3. Various plantings and their function

Planting no.	Utilitarian functions	Accompanying functions	Aesthetic functions	Type of planting[a]
1	to enclose a space to provide protection against the west wind to indicate ownership	to emphasize the drive	to create a rhythm to create a background	row of trees or shrubs
2	to separate two spaces to create a visual screen	to reinforce the row of trees or shrubs, and to give greater emphasis to the drive	to enhance the line of the drive	clipped hedge, 1.5m to 2m high
3	gardening, fruit growing	to accompany the drive	to create a background to balance the row of trees or shrubs	orchard planted in lines
4	—	to provide a transition between the orchard and the rest of the garden	to create a foreground for the view	shrubbery
5	to be a signal	to accompany the pergola	to punctuate the landscape of the garden to create a contrast with the horizontal structure of the pergola	specimen tree
6	—	to create a transition with the surrounding landscape, and therefore to integrate the garden into the terrain	to break up the view	shrubbery

7	to enclose the garden	to create a transition with the surrounding landscape, and therefore to integrate the garden into the terrain	to create a foreground for the view, without arresting the eye	informal mixed hedge, sometimes broadening out into clumps of bushes
8	to separate the southern part of the garden from the northern part to conceal the barn and the service entrance	to bring out the house, the old bakehouse, and the pond to serve as a transition with the surrounding landscape	to create a foreground for the view to create decorative effects (colors, shapes, etc.)	groups of trees behind shrubs and flowers
9	—	to accompany the house and terrace	to introduce a decorative note (colors) to bring out the building materials of the house (limestone) and of the terrace (schist) by separating them	flower beds
10	to separate the drive and parking area from the courtyard and garden	to enhance the building	to create an atmosphere of vegetation to create a volume with a certain transparency	shrubbery
11	to enclose the courtyard to create a screen against the northeast wind (infrequent but cold)	to provide a visual "cornerstone" to the entire property	to balance the various volumes	compact grove of trees

[a]This is the type of planting that, taken as a whole, seems most suited to all these functions, or at least to those that have been accorded a certain priority.

3. Third Stage: Choice of a Basic Plant

This choice is very important, for it will give the tone to our vegetal atmosphere. Indeed, we have sometimes chosen it, more or less consciously, while drawing the sketch, or while defining the atmosphere. In that case, we would have to check whether our first choice was well founded.

The basic plant must possess a number of very different qualities:

—It must clearly indicate the atmosphere chosen, without ambiguity, and must therefore be of a very "marked" type.
—It must form a transition with the terrain (if necessary, as here), and must therefore blend in well with the surrounding vegetation already in existence.
—It must be suitable for use in large numbers. Indeed, certain trees are best left in isolation as specimens, others are best in small groups. Our basic tree must be one that will be suitable for planting in broad masses.
—It must not be too decorative or too obtrusive (e.g., with colored foliage or picturesque in form). Indeed, in large masses, such a tree would be overwhelming, and would destroy the effects of the other plants.
—It must, of course, be particularly well adapted to the natural conditions.

In our example, we might choose a plant that already exists in the surrounding landscape: the ash. But taking into account the client's wish for a "rather old-fashioned, traditional style," we will choose instead the Dutch lime (*Tilia x euchlora* or *Tilia platyphyllos*), which seems to possess all the qualities mentioned above.

4. Fourth Stage: Choice of a "Family" of Plants

Thoroughly imbued as we now are with the chosen atmosphere, we can at this point go on and complete our list of plants.

What is required is, not to draw up an exhaustive list, but to jot down on a sheet of paper the names of those plants that come immediately to mind (as in the psychoanalytic technique of "free association").

The spontaneity and speed of this activity will give it a certain coherence, and excludes laborious researches in books, catalogs, etc., except with a view to checking up on certain forgotten details.

This presupposes, of course, an excellent knowledge of decorative plants!

Beginning with our basic plant—*Tilia x euchlora* or *Tilia platyphyllos*—we can go on, with a view to producing our chosen atmosphere, to a whole list of plants, suggesting both the ecological reference (the rural landscape) and the emotional reference (an elegant, sober garden, somewhat old-fashioned).

Fraxinus excelsior
Acer pseudoplatanus
Acer platanoïdes
Populus sp.
Malus sp.
Prunus sp.
Crataegus oxyacantha
Laburnum anagyroïdes
Alnus glutinosa
Alnus cordata
Fagus sylvatica
Spiraea x van houttei
Philadelphus coronarius
Paeonia suffruticosa
Deutzia sp.
Kerria japonica
Choisya ternata
Viburnum opulus
Ligustrum ovalifolium
Pyracantha sp.

Euonymus japonicus
Syringa vulgaris
Cornus alba
Sambucus nigra
Buxus sempervirens
Corylus avellana
Coronilla emerus
Catalpa bignonioïdes
Paulownia tomentosa
Hydrangea macrophylla
Hydrangea anomala var.
petiolaris
Liquidambar styraciflua
Liriodendron tulipifera
Chaenomeles x *superba*
Camellia japonica
Exochorda racemosa
Fuchsia magellanica
Hibiscus syriacus
Laurus nobilis
Species roses
perennial bedding plants (to
be decided on later)

5. Final Choice and Siting of the Plants

Let us go back to the list above. We now have a better idea of its weaknesses. For example, one might think that the decorative aspect of the garden might be lacking in winter, owing to inadequate numbers of evergreens, or that the number of summer flowering plants is too low, etc. One might also find it difficult to select a related "family" in order to create a slightly different atmosphere around the pond.

So we will have to go through that list again, eliminating some of the items. It is much too long: a garden or park is not an arboretum, but a coherent set of plants. So we shall eliminate those that seem farthest removed from our "family," and keep only those that meet our requirements exactly.

We may then have to add to it, in order to fill in the gaps. These new additions will, of course, have to fit in with the existing "family."

Experience teaches us not to use plants that we do not know. Before choosing them for our projects, it is always better to have observed them elsewhere, in similar situations.

After eliminations and additions, the revision of our list brings us to the placement of plantings listed in table 4.

The revision of our list is now complete, in accordance with the types of planting previously decided upon. All that remains is to plot these plants on the plan, (which we have done in fig. 64) with the aid of the letters in the final column of table 4.

Table 4.   Final choice of plants and their siting

Planting no.	Plant	Placement
1	*Tilia platyphyllos*	A
2	*Ligustrum ovalifolium*	B
3	*Malus x* (fruiting varieties)	C
	Pyrus x (fruiting varieties)	D
	Prunus x (fruiting varieties)	E
4	*Prunus avium* 'Plena'	F
	Malus pumila 'John Dawnie'	G
5	*Populus nigra* 'Italica'	H
6	*Prunus avium* 'Plena'	F
	Malus pumila 'John Dawnie'	G
	Salix alba 'Sericea'	I
7	*Spiraea x van houttei*	J
	Pyracantha coccinea 'Moretti'	
	Viburnum tinus	
	Ribes sanguineum 'King Edward VII'	
	Corylus avellana	
	Abelia x grandiflora	
	Escallonia x 'Uracladum'	
	Ligustrum ovalifolium	
	Crataegus oxyacantha 'Rosea Plena' (clump)	

Planting no.	Plant	Placement
8	*Photinia serrulata*	K
	Rhus typhina	L
	Pyrus salicifolia 'Pendula'	M
	Catalpa bignonioïdes	N
	Choisya ternata	O
	Pieris japonica	
	Acanthus mollis	
	Hosta sieboldiana	
	Helleborus niger	
	Pachysandra terminalis	
	Saxifraga crassifolia	
	Tradescantia virginiana	
	Iris kaempferi	
	Memerocallis flavis	
	Miscanthus Sinensis 'gracillimus'	
	Miscanthus saccharifolius	
9	*Rosa x* 'Queen Elizabeth'	P
10	*Liquidambar syraciflua*	Q
	Crataegus oxyacantha 'Rosea Plena' (standard)	R
	Magnolia grandiflora	S
	Acacia dealbata	T
	Laburnum anagyroïdes	U
	Tilia platyphyllos	A
11	*Tilia platyphyllos*	A

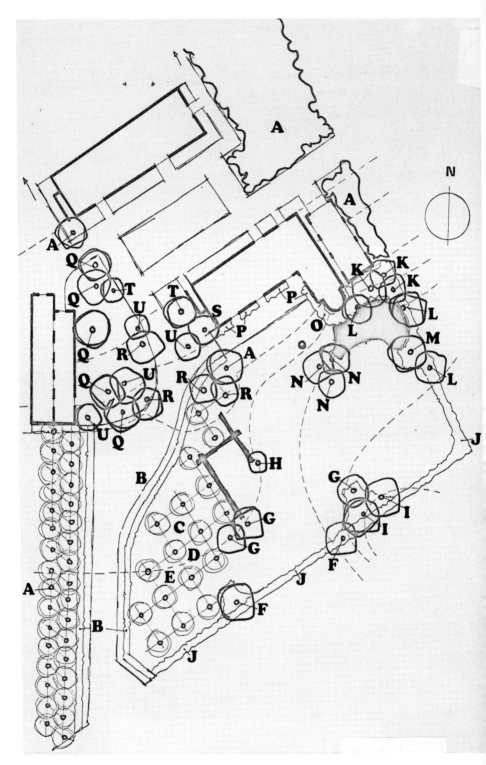

Fig. 64.   Final choice and siting of the plants.

III. Conclusion

We have tried to avoid the use of the word *beautiful* throughout our discussion of composition and planting. We have not done so because we think that a garden is above all "functional," and that nothing else really matters. On the contrary, we are convinced that its aesthetic qualities are very often a guarantee of good use and good survival, and that sometimes they are even sufficient justification for its existence. We have done so because the appreciation of the beautiful (or of its aesthetic qualities) follows rather than precedes a certain understanding, and this book has been an attempt to give a rational analysis of this understanding.

It is indeed curious to observe that Japanese gardens, which strike the profane by their very great aesthetic, spiritual, and symbolic qualities, are those that obey the greatest number of rules—rules that are so many "open sesames" for the initiate.

Rules are not enemies of the beautiful; on the contrary, they are necessary to achieving it—though not, of course, sufficient in themselves. Nevertheless, it is to be hoped that when materials like plants, with all their great qualities, are combined in a coherent composition, one is well on the way to attaining it.

IV. Alphabetical Index of Plants

The plants mentioned in the course of this book are often referred to by their vernacular names, where they exist, for the following reasons.

1. This book is intended for landscape gardeners, not for botanists.
2. This method allows for greater ease and immediacy of understanding.
3. In some of the examples used, there is no need to specify either the cultivar or even the species, but to cite only the genus, or even the type of plant. For example, sometimes we might wish to speak specifically of *Erica tetralix*, but sometimes we might speak of a carpet of heathers in general, which might very well include not only the Ericas but also the Callunas.

When no such vernacular name exists or when the term occurs in a list of a technical character, plants are given their Latin names.

The index below provides an alphabetical list of the Latin names of the plants referred to on pages 106–8, 129–30, 132–33 of this book.

C   *Calluna vulgaris*
    Camillia japonica
    Carex sp.
    Carpinus betulus
    Castanea sativa
    Catalpa bignonioïdes
    Chaenomeles x *superba*
    Chamaecyparis lawsoniana
        'Lanei'
    Choisya ternata
    Coronilla emerus
    Cornus alba
    Cornus sp.
    Corylus avellana
    Crataegus oxyacantha 'Rosea
        Plena'
    x *Cupressocyparis leylandii*
    Cupressus sempervirens 'Stricta'
    Cytisus scoparius

D   *Daboecia cantabrica*
    Deutzia sp.
    Dianthus barbatus

E   *Erica ciliaris*
    Erica cinerea
    Erica tetralix
    Escallonia x 'Uracladum'
    Euonymus japonicus
    Exachorda racemosa

F   *Fagus sylvatica*
    Festuca ovina 'Glauca'
    Filipendula ulmaria
    Forsythia sp.
    Fraxinus excelsior
    Fuchsia magellanica
        'Riccartoni'

G   *Genista anglica*
    Ginko biloba
    Gunnera chiliensis

H   *Hebe* x
    Hedera helix

Helleborus niger
Hemerocallis flava
Heracleum mantegazzianum
Hibiscus syriarus
Hosta sieboldiana
Hydrangea sp.
Hydrangea anomala var.
    petiolaris
Hydrangea macrophylla

I   *Iris* x *germanica*
    Iris kaempferi
    Iris laevigata
    Iris sibirica

J   *Juniperus chinensis* 'Pfitzeriana
        Aurea'
    Juniperus communis 'Hibernica'

K   *Kerria japonica*

L   *Laburnum anagyroïdes*
    Larix decidua
    Laurus nobilis
    Ligustrum ovalifolium
    Lilium sp.
    Liquidambar styraciflua
    Liriodendron tulipifera

M   *Magnolia grandiflora*
    Malus pumila 'John Dawnie'
    Malus x
    Memerocallus flavis
    Miscanthus sinensis
        'Gracillimus'
    Miscanthus saccharifolius
    Molinia coerulea

O   *Olea europaea*

P   *Pachysandra terminalis*
    Paeonia suffruticosa
    Paulownia tomentosa
    Philadelphus coronaria